NOBODY'S BOY

Ralph Harris

the Northern Connection

DARYL ASHBY

Ashby, Daryl, 1948-

For information contact:

Cover design by Daryl Ashby
Printed and bound in Canada by Crest Impressions,
Coquitlam, British Columbia, Canada

Paperback ISBN: 978-1-738-7075-0-8

FOREWORD

The media is fond of the phrase, "A usually quiet neighbourhood" when describing tragic events that often occur in what are truly peaceful communities. Indeed, most Canadian neighbourhoods offer a serenity that makes them enjoyable places to safely raise a family or live out the golden years without fear or anxiety.

However, some communities mask a more sinister underbelly, one that remains mostly unseen but exists nevertheless. And it is wicked and dangerous; a place where law-abiding citizens dare not venture.

Journalist and author Daryl Ashby is a master researcher, with an impressive ability to extract details of outrageous criminal behavior, injustice and intrigue from the characters who have participated in or been witness to activities that the average citizen is blissfully unaware.

Folks in the central part of Vancouver Island – including Ladysmith, Chemainus and Nanaimo – may have heard rumours of drug labs, outlaw bikers, unexplained disappearances, and unsolved murders, but until recently those stories were nothing more than tantalizing yarns with little substantive evidence that any of them were authentic.

Until recently.

In his popular 2018 book, 85 Grams, Daryl Ashby began to peel back the layers of mystery surrounding the life of Second World War hero, brilliant inventor and drug manufacturer and dealer Art Williams. It was illuminating for neighbours and the larger community who may have grown up with some knowledge of the legend of Williams but dismissed much of the banter as fantasies that grew in importance as they made the rounds in pubs and coffee shops.

Ashby shone a brilliant light on a dark world that only Williams' family, colleagues and the police knew existed. His research probed into a justice system that often failed, frequently outwitted by Williams and his criminal conspirators.

Now Daryl has upped the ante.

Art Williams was a genius. Dangerous and enigmatic. Ralph Harris was no Art Williams in intellect, but what he lacked in book smarts or technical ability, he more than made up for in brute strength, street smarts and charisma. An entrepreneur – albeit a dodgy one – Harris was dangerous. He survived and thrived in the most dangerous of realms, capable of protecting his interests with deadly force.

It has been said that every man's life contains sufficient material for a book. Some stories are more compelling than others and few can match the outrageous tales provided by the central character in Nobody's Boy, the notorious Ralph Harris.

For some, the lead character's moral code may be hard to swallow, but that doesn't alter the fact that his life produced sufficient material to justify being recorded within these pages.

This is a story about a man who defied the law, not so much for greed as was the case for many of his money-hungry associates, but for the steady infusion of adrenaline that raced through his veins.

Rather than align himself with an established criminal organization, he chose to navigate his own course

No one thought to abuse Ralph's loyalty or threaten those he held dear. To do so would be at their own peril. He was a man respected by his peers and in some cases, feared. For those who were slow to accept his ways, they would eventually realize, nothing would stand between him and his intended goal.

With a treasure trove of material gleaned from court documents and, most vital to the story, personal interviews with Harris shortly before his death, family members and scores of police officers, bikers, drug runners and others who shared Ralph's flamboyant life. Daryl Ashby has penned a book that exposes an underworld hereto undiscovered on Vancouver Island.

CHAPTER 1

He buried him deep, real deep, and that wasn't easy given the shallow amount of soil that covered the gravel and broken rock that dominated the shoulder of the abandoned logging road. To add insurance to his dig he tossed a heavy layer of the broken rock that fell to the side of the road over the site to discourage any four-legged predator from dragging the corpse to the surface, so a two-legged animal would see it.

As he neared the end of his life, Ralph Harris was more than comfortable sharing some of the deepest, darkest secrets of his colourful life.

"On Monday, April 26, 1993, Michael Edward Mickle, aka Zeke, came to my home in Ladysmith with one of his goons. Assuming he was paying me one more social visit, I invited him in. Had he informed me from the start that his sole purpose was to extort $20,000, I would have brushed him off at the door rather than offer him a complimentary joint or other form of hospitality.

"Zeke had been president of the Nanaimo chapter of the Hells Angels for some time and stated I owed the club money. I knew this was a crock as I never allowed myself to fall into arrears with the club. I'm smart enough to know it's not good for one's health.

"Anyone who's crazy enough to dance with those boys learns quickly that if you screw with them, it will be your last tango. I knew he was just blowing smoke so I told him as much, then suggested in less than polite terms how he could close the front door behind him. The bottom line is there was no way he was going to get a nickel out of me that he didn't earn."

In reality, the word on the streets suggested Zeke owed the club a ton of money from a cocaine deal that went off the rails, so having a shortlist of those he could muscle, he figured he would start with Ralph Ross Harris, as he was viewed as having deep pockets and an easy target. That was mistake number one.

Ralph had a strong suspicion Zeke wouldn't take his refusal well, so he wasn't surprised when Zeke and a buddy resorted to their tried and tested method of persuasion. Zeke was the first to start laying his fists, laden with a row of heavy rings, into Ralph's head. His buddy soon joined in with little to no regard for the outcome.

By the time they were finished, Ralph's left eye had closed from the bruising while the flesh around it wept from a series of deep cuts. His lip on the same side looked like it had succeeded in overdosing on collagen as the pair did their best to loosen a few of his teeth. In short, he looked like George Chuvalo after Smokin' Joe Frazier finished him off in their 1967 bout. But just like Chuvalo, Ralph remained on his feet until Zeke had finished showing him just how tough he was.

What Zeke didn't know, was that Ralph had been entertaining a friend when the duo arrived. The young lady wisely remained hidden behind the partially closed bedroom door as she knew recognition would not prove to her benefit no matter what the purpose of their visit. As it was, she heard every word and witnessed the horror of the beating.

"As soon as Zeke and his goon had left, Ralph swore to me that Zeke 'was a dead man'. He had already proven himself to be a man who never made idle threats, so I was convinced he meant what he said," the woman recalled years later.

On April 30, 1993, the Nanaimo RCMP received word that 56-year-old Edward "Zeke" Mickle, president of the Nanaimo Hells Angels, had returned from a trip to Vancouver where he had picked up a couple of the club's ceremonial death head rings and then he vanished. An initiation event was planned for the evening where two prospects were to receive their full colours along with the club ring. Such events are important to all club members.

All anyone knew was that Zeke's truck was found parked on the east side of the Harewood Arms Pub in Nanaimo, locked, with no keys to be found.

Within hours, the cops' wire taps were humming as members of the local chapter exchanged threats of war against any man or group responsible for his disappearance. There was so much phone chatter that it was clear they had no idea who may have offed their leader. With more zeal than the authorities, they were scrambling for clues, anything that would put a face to the act.

The bikers had so many theories to run with, ranging from a personal debt long overdue, to inter-club ill feelings, to a jilted lover. Taking Zeke out was something almost anyone could do if they got the drop on him but making him disappear is something else altogether. He was a big man, a solid 260 pounds.

Fitting him with concrete slippers would have taken a team of men with above average strength. The same could be said for manoeuvring him out of a vehicle and into a hole some distance off the beaten track. It could have been two individuals who worked together in taking him down but as they say, "the only way to keep a secret when two or more are involved, is if all but one are rendered unable to talk."

Coincidentally, the cops had seen two heavyweights from back east milling about the bikers' clubhouse on Old Victoria Road in Nanaimo that same week. It was assumed they were demanding repayment of the money that Zeke owed them on an investment that had gone south.

Whether the cops made a sincere effort to locate Zeke's whereabouts three decades ago will never be revealed but it's general knowledge the RCMP won't invest a whole lot of time trying to locate one of the boys or one of their puppet members when they go missing. As long as it's a situation not involving an innocent bystander, the cops view it as resolution by attrition. Until now, only a handful of Ralph's close confidants have known the truth behind what really happened that night.

Here's how it went down. Ralph knew if he walked up and stuck a gun to Zeke's head, within a millisecond a battle would be on. Zeke would never go down without a fight and he was not the type of character you wanted to go hand to hand with. So, on the afternoon of April 30, 1993 while Zeke was returning from the Mainland, Ralph arranged to meet him at one of the club's favourite watering holes to square away their differences.

Zeke bought the tale, hook, line and sinker. Ralph waited patiently as he watched Zeke drive off the Departure Bay ferry at 3:25 p.m., then followed at a discrete distance until he pulled into the parking lot of the Harewood Arms. The pub was where everyone was your friend until they were not; where things are quiet until they are deafening and it's a place where you can drink away whatever life throws at you. On this gloomy, late April afternoon it was unusually quiet.

As Zeke exited his truck, Ralph pulled up alongside, offering him his passenger door. The rain had been pelting down for the better part of the day, so even Zeke found little to no difficulty at interpreting the message as 'climb in, sit down and let's get this over with'.

As if on cue, he did just that. Ralph removed his foot from the brake, turning slowly onto Eighth Street driving west to Howard, then north to Seventh Street, which eventually transitioned into the Harewood Mines Road.

The two men exchanged small talk until Zeke insisted on knowing what Ralph had in mind. By then they were well beyond the residential core and some distance along the Nanaimo Lakes Road.

To disarm Zeke's imagination, Ralph drove with a slight twist in his body towards his passenger and his right arm extended over the back of the seat. He told Zeke he had $15,000 in the glove box and it was all he could muster at the moment, but he would do his best to procure more.

Zeke was already bending to open the box, so it was unlikely he heard anything further. He likely thought he had died and gone to heaven. What he didn't know was that he was definitely going to die. But as for his afterlife, that is any man's guess.

Prior to pulling into the pub parking lot Ralph had wedged his cocked Ruger .22 pistol between his left shoulder blade and the seat. As Zeke leaned over, fully engrossed in pulling the thick envelope from the compartment, Ralph casually reached back, brought his gun forward and popped two slugs into the back of Zeke's head.

Zeke rolled forward into a fetal position oozing only a small amount of blood on the rubber floor mat. An easy clean.

Ralph was only a mile or so from the many abandoned logging roads that lead off into the hills north of Nanaimo River Road. He had already staked out one that would be suitable for disposing of a corpse. It would be no time before he was back home, worry free.

If you are the emotional type, Ralph suggested after telling his story, don't waste a tear for the dead man as he had played judge, jury and executioner on more occasions than one should care to remember. Even though he preached the doctrine of family and brotherhood within the club, he took the lives of a couple of his brothers for reasons far more trivial than this.

"Rather than keeping the club and its members front and centre, Zeke's motives had always been geared towards personal power and financial gain," Ralph claimed.

"It was some time later I found out the cops had previewed the tapes from the gas station security cameras next door to the pub. By some stroke of luck, I had slipped in and out of the parking lot between frames."

Word on the street aligned with the suggestion the loss of Zeke may be the community's gain. Regardless, the authorities knew there was going to be hell to pay in the fallout. The Nanaimo chapter figured this was an issue between themselves and a conflicting club, an insult that required retaliation. Hints of an all-out war were bantered from every bar stool in town.

The British Columbia Hells Angels chapters are the wealthiest in all of Canada and possibly the entire world. This reality did not evolve by sheer luck, but rather on the backs of hardworking individuals such as Ralph Harris who became one of the primary growers of marijuana in the Pacific Northwest.

To be clear, no club is wealthy as a whole, but rather, a select few within it. Ralph Harris provided a sizable source of revenue for certain members since the late 1960s and Zeke had been a principal beneficiary.

He along with others had encouraged Ralph a number of times to take up their patch and enjoy the benefits of the club. In Ralph's mind he already had access to their binge socials and when it came to their drugs, he had enough pot of his own to last a lifetime. As for the heavier drugs, they weren't his thing.

Then there were the nickel and dime whores who frequented the club only to navigate beneath the hungry boys in exchange for a quick fix. By the time they were passed through the rank and file to reach him, they would be bruised, sweaty and lifeless. The kindest thing he could do for them would be to stand them up in front of a pressure washer. Besides, why would he want them when he had his own bevy of perfect 10s with no prerequisite to share? While club members act independently when it comes to their illicit activities, Ralph maintained that he never condoned commercial prostitution or the degenerate activities that flow with it.

"While I may leave an audience ample room to question my moral code, I have always drawn this line clearly in the sand and done my best to live within it."

There were times when Ralph came close to yielding to their invitation, especially during the all-night binge parties where the liquor flowed as freely as the girls, or when he would ride in a testosterone fueled pack of a dozen or more bikers at white-knuckle speeds while holding a tight formation. Had any one of the boys blown a tire or lost their focus, the highway carnage would have been immeasurable. But once his head cleared of all the nonsense, he remained strong as ever to survive as 'Nobody's Boy'. Having said that, he emphasized, "If I were asked to do something for the club's hierarchy, they were able to consider it done. What's more, I kept my mouth shut. That is until now," Ralph explained when, shortly before his death, he opened up about his life in a series of candid interviews.

The bikers' admin are not only control freaks but sticklers for detail. They have their puppet clubs or 'triple layering' as it's referred to, where the dirty work is carried out by someone well removed from those carrying a flaming death head patch. This level of insulation makes it nearly impossible for law enforcement to gain a conviction of a patched member.

"Not being an official member of any layer, I was able to complete tasks for them while offering even greater impunity."

The club holds dear to being one percenters, a term coined at Hollister, California in 1947 by a group who considered themselves rebels as they remained glued to the saddles of their bikes during waking hours. As a general rule, the club members of today may still fit into the 'rebel' category, but they often move about on four wheels, while two wheels are reserved for symbolic rides.

Their patch or colours, as they refer to them are actually three parts and consist of a centre portion which denotes the club logo, a curved top rocker identifying the club by name, and the bottom rocker which denotes their affiliation by city, province or state.

Only the full-fledged members wear all three, while those under consideration are referred to as prospects and carry only the lower rocker.

Determined to be his own man, Ralph Harris saw little appeal in joining the Hells Angels.

"I had no interest in being a prospect, which is nothing more than a glorified gofer on call 24/7. If I went this route, I would be expected to chauffeur full-patched members around and play bodyguard, or make deliveries of contraband, guns, and women, for nothing more than slave labour. Prospects, like hang-arounds, get savage beatings if they foul up. That would be no picnic."

Surviving the prospect or hang-around phase requires you to be on call and respond promptly if the leadership sees fit. This position could last for years while all the time doing their dirty work and gaining little to no respect in return.

He saw himself as more valuable as an outsider, prepared to do whatever needed to be done for the club.

"I was their meal ticket. They needed me more than I needed them.

Fact is, the admin tend not to pay their own way at events, often leaving the prospect with no choice but to pick up the tab."

A newbie is first considered a hang-around. If they live long enough to please the leadership through their actions or by being a good earner, they might be rewarded with the lower rocker of the club colours. This is where the status of prospect comes into play. All this would have accomplished would be to push Ralph up a notch. He would still have had to work security on runs or meetings, plus serve drinks at their many parties between running errands.

Most underlings quit, end up dead or wind up serving time. Very few ever earn their full patch. The cops are constantly monitoring them just because of their association.

"I didn't need that kind of heat." The ultimate outcome of Ralph's decision was, "Thanks, but no thanks. I will remain nobody's boy until the day I die."

Bikers are a contradiction onto themselves. They profess to be anti-authoritarian, nonconformists, yet they dress the same and invoke some of the strictest rules of any organization. Their very name and logo are trademarked, as they consider their group to be a secret society, yet again they are exhibitionists when they promote T-shirt sales and toy runs for the less fortunate. Their very existence is a contradiction onto itself.

The Hells Angels insists on its members attending their weekly meetings which they refer to as 'church'. Each member has to place the interests of the club above all else, including their wives, family, and employment, while following well-defined protocol, the likes of which would stymie the average man's independence.

"In short, anything I chose to do within my own business that might affect the club had to be first approved by the senior executive. Had the club discovered that I wasted their prez, patch or no patch, it would not have been pretty."

The cardinal rule with the bikers is: If you mess with one of their boys, you will answer to all of them. The ultimate revenge would have been extracted against the man who took the life of one of the brothers, let alone their president. After they had abused the culprit in every way imaginable, they would inflict on him the utmost of pain, for as long as the individual had a will to draw air into his lungs, and only then, would they dispatch him to whatever eternity he had waiting for him.

With Zeke's unsolved execution lingering in the background, Ralph was never tempted to reckon with the bikers' morbid ritual of revenge. So, he decided to take that story to his death, which peacefully came his way uninvited, yet by natural causes, during the night of December 5, 2017.

From the grave, perhaps he would offer kudos to the two club members who paid his ex-wife a visit following the funeral. They were straight up guys who expressed their regrets, saying Ralph was the real deal; a man who they could trust and respect. Mind you, that was long before they had had an opportunity to read his memoirs.

As for the lady who was sharing Ralph's bed on the night Zeke came to visit, the words of Benjamin Franklin come to mind: "If you would keep your secret from an enemy, tell it not to a friend."

While that may be the case, Ralph never gave her potential betrayal a second thought as he trusted her more than most he'd taken into his confidence. And there weren't many. They had been together off and on for over twenty years, but during his later years he had developed issues with his eyes causing his driver's license to be revoked, which in turn limited his ability to come and go. So, entertaining any former pleasures with her or others became nearly impossible. As they say, when the grass on one side of a fence dries up, the cattle simply move onto greener pastures.

Harewood Arms Pub.

Ceremonial Death Head Rings.

Harewood Arms Pub Aerial View.

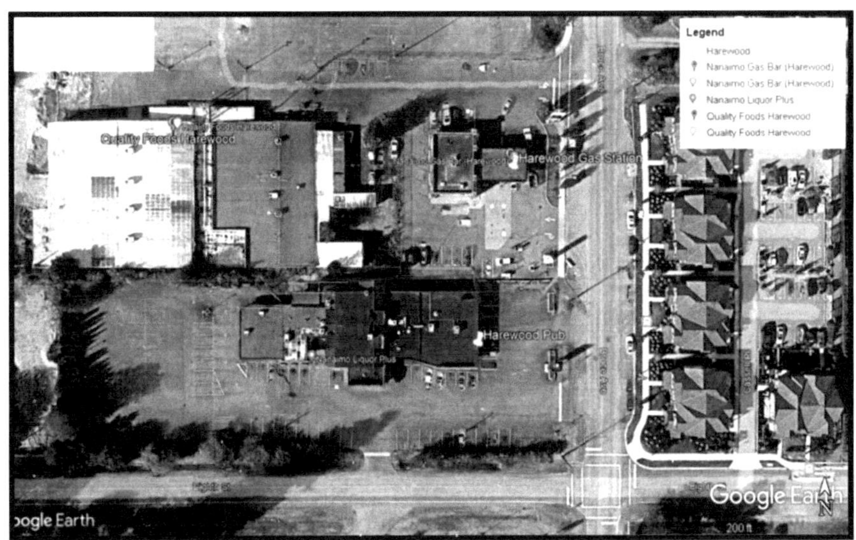

Early Image - Nanaimo Chapter of the 101 Knights.

101 Knights after they patched over to the Hells Angels.

CHAPTER 2

For many of you, this is your first introduction to Ralph Ross Harris.

Some of those who knew him, referred to him as 'White Hair' but never to his face for reasons you will come to understand in the coming chapters. Others, who were somewhat closer, were able to get away with calling him 'Cornflakes' for reasons that were never explained.

Prior to his passing, Ralph invited me to record his life story. He did however grant this blessing with one proviso: "For those of you who I have shared a sin or two and are still enjoying life, not to worry, I have no intention of exposing you here.

"I expect you will be shocked by some of my confessions, so lean back and see if you can figure out just how you fit into each of my dirty deeds, without fear of reprisal."

As the writer who has been granted a glimpse into Ralph's secret life, I intend to honour his wishes to the best of my ability.

Ralph was born September 22, 1939, in the small town of Chemainus, about 75 miles north of Victoria, British Columbia and about midpoint between Duncan and Ladysmith. Its population still hovers around the 3,900 mark. Everyone knows everyone and trying to keep secrets is a lost cause. They say if you dial a wrong number in Chemainus, the community is so small you could still end up talking for fifteen minutes.

He had two sisters, one his senior and the other younger. His eldest sister passed away in 2018. I won't be mentioning their names as this story is not going to sit well with their legacy and they deserve their privacy. Having said that, they were never ignorant as to how Ralph often managed to display a quarter million dollars on his kitchen counter. But speaking of such notoriety today would only bring them reproach in the eyes of their peers.

The area's primary source of employment since the early 1950s has been the nearby Crofton pulp mill with its deep seaport. But like many other things within that community, it is sometimes a struggle to remain viable. The mill has changed hands frequently over the years and has managed to survive despite other mill closures on Vancouver Island.

Ralph's parents, Ross and Betty were the most caring and giving individuals you could ever hope to meet. They were never harsh towards their kids and as a family it could never be said they were dysfunctional. Ralph inherited his mother's shortened stature, plus her thick black hair, but from his father came the broad shoulders and barrel chest.

His dad owned Modern Sash & Door at the south end of Chemainus.

Ralph remembered a man by the name of O'Shea walking into his father's shop in 1957. The guy had literally just gotten off the boat, having sailed from Britain in search of a new life for his family and he was desperate for work.

"Dad looked him up and down and concluded he would make a good worker, so he gave him a job. The guy had a family of six with no place to stay, so mom rearranged my sisters' and my sleeping quarters, then moved the whole lot of them into our home, ensuring no one went hungry."

Ralph was not unlike his parents in that regard as he often gave money to those who appeared to be in need, without expectations of repayment. Equally so, there were occasions when he offered credit to an individual who knew from the start that he would exact the agreed upon repayment by one means or another. Most who knew him considered Ralph not only just, but also a stern businessman. To those who considered him weak or who neglected to take sufficient time to comprehend his business ethics he remained an enigma.

Working as a kid in his dad's shop, Ralph discovered he had a natural affinity to seamlessly marry two pieces of wood together, but the craft wasn't enough to hold his attention. To the day of his passing he pondered why he could not have settled into his father's business. It would have offered him a secure income and a sizable nest egg upon retirement. The only explanation appears to be that such work was unable to take him to that edge, which his inner spirit craved.

Ralph was an average student in school and while he stood his ground if someone started to throw their weight around, he was never known as a scrapper. He never hung with a specific group but went off and did his own thing.

"Most everyone I knew in my youth smoked dope. Like so many others, I dropped a tablet of acid but I found it unsettling when I lost control of my movements and those decisions that needed to be made. So I chose not to use it again. With no theatre or rink in town there was little else to do but joints, girls and create as much mayhem as possible.

"Pot was as easy to find as beer. The choice of the day was not whether you were going to smoke pot or not, but rather were you going to do pot or drink beer. It came down to the individual and what they considered to be a prerequisite to a party."

As kids, those that drank generally played sports, listened to loud music and danced, while those that smoked seldom became the prom king or queen. They listened to loud music as well, but rather than dance, they talked about local or national issues. While Ralph was predisposed to become a smoker, he was not much of a talker. In contrast he became a good listener.

While still in high school, Ralph started growing a small amount of pot for his own use.

"I purchased a bag of birdseed from the local hardware store then sifted out the marijuana seeds for my starter kit. When those first plants came to maturity, I allowed some to go to seed so I would have ample for the crops that followed."

Ralph was producing such a sweet, mellow high, that friends began asking for his product rather than risk being caught buying from the local pusher. That guy was well known by the authorities, while Ralph managed to move around beneath their radar.

This was the pivotal moment when Ralph's life shifted 180 degrees and morphed from the boy next door into the man who had been at odds with the law for over fifty years.

"My parents would have been horrified if they knew what I had been up to. They weren't church going people but they definitely lived by a moral code well removed from that which I have chosen."

To ensure they remained in the dark during his younger years, Ralph raised his plants in a forested area across the highway from where he lived. Logging roads ran up the south side of Mt. Brenton providing access to mossy outcrops that offered great sun yet removed from prowling eyes. His plants were started in eight-inch plastic pots, which were easy to come by, plus cheap enough to abandon when no longer needed. Grow-ops were not commonplace so no one thought to ask why he was buying them.

In the early days, the RCMP didn't use choppers to crisscross the countryside looking for pot plants like they do today, so he was able to relax with little to no fear of detection.

His venture was one of the first on the local scene since most of the product people smoked came from Mexico or overseas at considerable expense. With little to no overhead, Ralph was able to put out some potent weed and realize a sizable profit.

When volume was the order of the day, Ralph purchased a kitchen garbage compactor from Sears and compressed the weed into tightly compacted kilo packages. This all changed when the bud became the market of choice. Buyers didn't want to see the life of their precious flower crushed beyond recognition.

"A lot of grass was being imported from Mexico; that is up until the CIA started spraying the farms with Paraquat. Then it started coming from California. I remember when the first pot arrived with no seeds. They shipped it in gallon jars with buyers acting like it was gold-plated. The following year Mexican weed was all but history."

CHAPTER 3

Social turmoil invaded every household in one form or another during the 1960s. The media presented the Vietnam War like a mini-series while the assassination of Martin Luther King, President John F. Kennedy and Bobby Kennedy shocked the very foundation of society. Our world seemed to be on the brink of disaster.

On the local scene, biker clubs started tearing up the asphalt of Vancouver Island highways. As with every organization, the strong and determined rose to the top. In the Island's case this was the 101 Knights, a ragtag group of sixteen hardcore one percenters, as they preferred to be known.

They were a blend of personalities and physicalities, but one common denominator they shared was the lust to ride and the desire to prosper.

Today, those same individuals would be difficult to pick out of a crowd of Wall Street brokers or accountants. They have come a long way in recognizing the benefit of social hygiene, clean attire, and branding for the sake of business structure, it would seem.

Well over 50 years have passed since the first outlaw bikers migrated from Powell River to the Island, with a number of the young men now pushing up daisies by natural and unnatural causes. Others are quietly reveling in their retirement (some granted – some forced), yet still a handful are discretely enjoying their senior years while wearing today's flaming head across their backs.

Three of the original members still hold council within British Colombia chapters and each do so with the well-earned authority unequaled by their peers.

During the '60s, one by one, they stripped the other clubs of their colours and banished them from their turf. The only hold-out referred to themselves as The Bounty Hunters. These fellows held court in a rundown turn-of-the-century home on Hillside Avenue in Victoria, where President Eddie Henry Eng, or Woo Fat as he was better known, held firm control of the reins.

Woo Fat made it known he was not going to drop his colours no matter who asked. This left but one option, a personal visit by the 101 Knights.

When the 101 Knights arrived at the Bounty Hunter's clubhouse, two Victoria police black and whites were parked outside. One of the officers stepped out of his car and insisted on knowing what business they had with the Victoria group. "Social," they replied.

Once inside they discovered the cops had been waiting for one of the Hunters to exit so he could be arrested on an outstanding warrant.

With Eddie Eng still refusing to relinquish his colours, the Knights went to work applying physical persuasion. In short order the last of the Hunters tossed his vest into a pile on the floor, whereupon the pile was taken to the rear yard of the building and lit ablaze with the help of some lighter fluid.

When the fellow who the cops were waiting for exited the clubhouse, his face displayed substantial disfigurement and prompted the question as to how he got such a beating. "I fell in the bathroom while trying to take a piss," was his surly reply.

With their mission accomplished and the cops long gone, the 101 Knights returned north to Nanaimo and continued to expand their business interests. With the retirement of the Bounty Hunters, the 101 Knights motorcycle gang controlled the majority of the drugs flowing throughout Vancouver Island and into the Lower Mainland. With Ralph Harris maintaining control of the Island's pot supply, the club hierarchy insisted on being dialed into Ralph's operation.

They were a long-haired motley crew in the '60s and '70s, a time when personal hygiene was considered non-essential to their lifestyle. The hardened grease on their jeans gave testament to the number of times their Harleys needed roadside repair. But all that changed in 1983 when they patched over to the Satan's Choice, as a prerequisite to stitching the Hells Angels flaming death head onto their leather vests.

From that day on, they adopted a semi-professional look which could easily blend into the nine-to-five crowd. But under that spotless veneer, they were clearly open for business.

Unlike the '70s and '80s, policing today is designed to hire recruits who are unable to think for themselves. They are just pawns to parade before the masses and exert as much muscle and power as needed to keep the good folk in line.

Those who wear a patch on their backs or a tattoo defining them as a member of a particular club aren't the least bit intimidated. They carry on business with near impunity.

"I did all I could over the years to remain a nondescript character within the local community by dealing with only those who had more to lose than me if and when the hammer came down," stated Harris.

Although he was well-known by people in and around Ladysmith, few knew how the low-key Ralph Harris filled his after hours. "I never drove a flashy car, nor would I wear gold chains or jewelry as that would only call attention. When under the public's microscope, I carried myself like everyone else.

"In my youth I never saw myself as a violent man with a hair-trigger temper. Having said that, I always lived by the principle that those who mess with my family or close friends will, whether they want to or not, come to know me in a more personal way and to do so is at your own peril."

One year, seventeen-year-old Ralph was hunting with a younger cousin in the Horne Lake area. They had moved together through the woods to where they split up following a horseshoe shaped ridge, walking in opposite directions. This gave them the advantage of sweeping the upper level of the ridge and the valley floor at the same time.

"We moved at about the same pace when we hunted so our plan was to meet somewhere in the middle and then work out where we would go from there. If either of us heard a shot, we'd assume the other got his deer and we would link up in the kill zone."

As Ralph reached their anticipated point of rendezvous, his cousin was nowhere to be found. Thinking the fellow may have been moving slower than himself, he kept to the circular route, while crossing his fingers his cousin would verify any movement in the bush before he squeezed the trigger.

"I could hear this faint moaning of a child in discomfort. As I came around a rock outcrop there was my cousin pinned over a log with some big dude astride him from the back sodomizing him with all his energy."

Ralph's natural instinct was to turn defender, so the rage that followed could have been anticipated. The guy was so engrossed in his physical gratification that he didn't hear Ralph walk up behind him. The first hint that things weren't right was when the guy felt the cold steal from the muzzle of Ralph's rifle pressed firmly into his left ear. He didn't have time to register what was about to happen as Ralph pulled the trigger.

The hollow-point round mushroomed as it entered his brain at 3,600 feet per second and exited the far side of the guy's skull taking with it a volume of pink brain matter along with close to half the right side of his skull. It sprayed across the moss like some abstract buffet served up to every insect within a mile.

"My cousin was so badly shaken, he didn't realize the fellow was no longer on him. He just fell limp onto the log sobbing hysterically."

While he regained his senses, Ralph dragged what was left of the pervert into the waist deep shalal, where he'd remain hidden for the time being.

"I made it clear. My cousin was to put the entire event behind him and never to speak of it, which to the best of my knowledge remains the case to this day."

In hindsight, perhaps Ralph did the guy a favour, as the penal system would not have been so kind. In all likelihood he would have continued bastardizing every young boy or girl he dominated until one day the system caught up to him.

Then he would go through a lengthy trial and appeal process until his options ran out, all the time dragging his family name through the media. If the system worked, he would face a lengthy duration of incarceration. At least that is how it should work. In reality, those hardcore inmates already serving time take a dim view of pedophiles and assume it's their duty to purge the penal system of their kind.

While our guy stood in absolute horror, a couple of inmates would hold him while another would drive a shiv deep into each armpit severing the primary blood flow to each limb. There he would bleed out in a matter of minutes while his executioners vanished back into the prison's general population.

There are no cameras in prison showers as that would go against the convict's human rights. So no record of what transpired would ever be recorded. An act cleanly yet painfully executed, ridding society of yet one more scourge upon the earth.

As dreadful a fate as what this might appear, the horror he faced during his final moments would never equal the emotional trauma Ralph's cousin endured for the rest of his natural life.

Bounty Hunters at their clubhouse in Victoria.

CHAPTER 4

Yvonne Dryer grew up a mile down the road from Ralph's home. "In school I was her senior by two and a half years, so she was graduating into my school as I was completing my final year. Yvonne was a popular girl with all the boys even though word had it she wasn't easy. Yet there was something about her that held my eye, long before she knew I existed," Ralph recalled during one interview that covered a period in his life some fifty years earlier.

Though her lack of height may have left others wanting, with Ralph's own stature somewhat stunted, he considered her a perfect fit. As a bonus, she was easy on the eyes and had a personality that made her a breeze to get along with. Or so he thought.

Ralph's preferred mode of transportation dating back to his youth had been a half-ton pickup. In the sixties they came with a bench seat long enough to hold a party. Yvonne and he weren't dating long before they found the recreational benefit of the truck's front seat.

Back then, it seemed most girls around Chemainus were or had been pregnant at one point or another. So the youth never got their knickers in a knot over what the community thought of them being sexually involved prior to marriage. Fact is, a girl getting pregnant was as routine as going to the movies today.

After a brief courtship Ralph and Yvonne tied the knot in April of 1958.

"Yvonne made it known during our first years together that I was 'a good man, a good father and a consistent provider'. She also suggested I was 'gregarious, private and introspective.'

"Our first son was born before our ninth month of marriage, but for the record, I never married her because I had to. I did it because I wanted to. Regardless, the little guy passed away within a few days of his birth and it was then that I discovered just how divisive Yvonne's mother could be.

"Regardless of everything working against us, before I fell out of favor with Yvonne, we managed to coexist for six years and produce three beautiful healthy children; one boy and two girls."

Yvonne's mother never made it a secret that she held Ralph in low esteem and declared him well below the social ladder her daughter should have attracted as a spouse. She made this painfully clear at their wedding, prophesying that Yvonne would become terribly unhappy and regret the day she ever met him.

"I believe her mom was recasting the drama that surrounded her own marriage and the life that ensued. As it was, I swore she was high on something during our wedding after-party. She definitely had an issue with balance and would laugh with a high-pitched cackle for no apparent reason, and then moan like a banshee as though her appendix was about to burst. The entire evening, she jockeyed from one extreme to another."

With the birth of their son on December 13, 1958, her mother overpowered anyone who got in her way and took control of the child the moment he was born, whisking him out of Yvonne's arms and into the hospital nursery, never to be returned. At her insistence the hospital staff kept the nursery curtains closed and the door into the nursery locked.

When they did learn of their son's passing, Ralph and Yvonne were told it was the result of galloping pneumonia. Just the same, Yvonne and Ralph were kept in the dark long enough to ensure neither had an opportunity to say their goodbyes. No matter how many times they enquired as to his state of health, they received no reply until the day before his funeral. That too, her mother orchestrated with as much control as a military drill sergeant.

On the day of the funeral, Yvonne's mother showed up with a doctor the newlyweds had never met. On her mother's instruction, the doctor gave Yvonne a shot which he said was to calm her nerves, when in fact it knocked her out completely, causing her to miss the proceedings altogether.

Yvonne's mother was an attractive woman but that is where the similarity ended between her and her daughter. While Yvonne's father was well-liked by everyone who knew him, her mother rewrote the definition of evil.

Ralph learned somewhat late in their relationship that she had a well-defined nymphomaniac disorder. The fact that she had an uncontrollable bent to parade herself about town as the local slut was not a secret within the community, but rather the fodder for every kitchen table following Sunday services.

When ships tied up at the Crofton Mill, Yvonne's mother would disappear from the home for hours. Oftentimes she could be seen leaning against the bar at the local pub rubbing more than elbows with a complete stranger. It got to a point where she would be gone for entire weekends with no attempt to explain her absence when she finally returned.

Yvonne endured many atrocities during her childhood. From the age of four, Yvonne's mother passed her around the community to every degenerate she sought favour with.

"I remember it all so clearly now," Yvonne recalls. "There are times when I wish I didn't, but I can't undo what is already done."

One horrific incident stands out in her mind and decades later she was able to remember very specific details.

"It started out like every other day. As soon as Dad left for work, Mom spent a great deal of time on her clothes, hair and makeup, then she dressed me in one of my nicest dresses and brushed my hair until my ringlets were almost straight. It is so fresh in my mind, as though it just happened yesterday.

"Mom always dressed me as though she was still a little girl herself and playing dress-up, only I was her doll. I see clearly the frilly dress with the bright red floral pattern on it. It had one of those collars that itched like crazy. It had short sleeves and it was gathered at the waist, flowing from there out into billows, trimmed with lace. During my happier moments I would spin to the music that played in my head causing it to float up in the air like a cloud.

"After we were both ready, I would normally tag along as she set out to fulfill all the errands she had for herself, but unlike other days, mother had something sinister in store for me.

"To this day I have no idea why mother took me to that house, nor why she left me with that man. I knew from the moment I saw him that he was not nice and I remember the feeling in the pit of my stomach, even at that young age that his intentions were not good, at least towards me.

"Mother took me by the hand and led me inside the front door of his house, then whispered something in his ear so soft I couldn't hear. Then she bent down far enough to look me straight in the eye and said she would be back in an hour or so to pick me up. She looked at the man again and threw him a faint smile.

"She never kissed me goodbye, but that was not unusual. She just left. I could hear the heels from her shoes click, clack down the concrete path to the car, the door to her car open and then close, the car start and then fade to quiet as she drove off along the gravel road.

"There was a deep fear growing inside me, but I really didn't know why. This man was not my grandfather because I knew he still lived in England and I was confident he was not one of my uncles. To the best of my knowledge, he had never been to our house as I would have remembered the deep pots engraved in his face. For that same reason, I felt certain he had never been to any of the parties my parents attended.

"It wasn't until the light from the front door vanished that I realized just how dark it was in that room. If it wasn't for a few strands of sun stealing their way between the folds of the window curtains, the room would be completely void of colour.

"The man didn't say a word, he just reached down, took my right hand, and squeezed it tight. His hand was dry unlike my mother's or for that matter my father's. There was no tenderness in the way he gripped mine. I could feel each callous rubbing against the skin on the back of my hand and it reminds me today of coarse sandpaper.

"He pulled me along towards the back of his home. We went into the kitchen with its unswept floors and dirty dishes stacked haphazardly on the counter. There was a strong odor of rotten food rising up from the metal cat dish on the floor. I thought he couldn't be that bad of a man if he had a cat, but I didn't see a cat anywhere.

"I figured he was going to feed me something but we didn't stop in the kitchen, he just walked towards another door off to the side. As he opened the door, again there was no light, but I could make out the foot of a bed and a few pieces of underwear and socks lying on the floor. He didn't turn on a light but once my eyes had adjusted to the din, I could see quite clearly this was the room he slept in.

"There was the odd piece of dark furniture, but mostly there was just the bed. It wasn't overly big, about the same size as mine I guess, just longer. The blankets were messed up. As I looked back to where we had come from, the light from the kitchen allowed me to see more than I wanted.

"He let go of my hand and I just stood there not knowing what to do. He started to unclasp his belt all the time looking down at me with a sinister grin. The noise from the large buckle filled the room. That was followed by the sound of a zipper. He said nothing to me while his pants fell to the floor, he just reached down and put his hands under my arms and lifted me up onto the side of his bed. I just sat there as he worked his underwear down his long hairy legs and then kicked them off to the side with all the others.

"I never had a brother and there were no little boys that lived around our house during my early years so I never came to know what a boy should look like by normal inquisitive means; let alone that of a grown man. I never gave it a lot of thought at that age, but I just assumed little boys were made much the same as little girls. But I could see clearly that this was not the case. His thing was dark in the dim light and it was fat and pointing towards me. Even in my innocence I knew it looked evil and menacing.

"He just stood there and looked at me with the same sickening smirk in the corner of his mouth. Then he reached over with both hands and pushed me back down onto his bed. I felt him reach up under my pretty dress. He started pulling on my panties and he kept tugging at them until they slid off my legs. I was already feeling sick and wanted to cry out, but I was too frightened to do anything.

"Why did Mommy leave me there? Did she not know what this man was going to do?

"He pushed his naked body up between my legs. I wanted to tell him to stop but the words never found their way to my lips. It felt like I was burning inside, it hurt so bad. A tear formed in the corner of my eye, then another and another, until they ran freely down the side of my cheek. Still, no words came to my lips. I could feel him inside me, and he kept hurting me as he did what he wanted to do, again and again.

"I was just a little girl. I had never hurt anyone, and I know with all certainty, I had never done anything to anger him. I didn't even know his name and I needed my mommy to watch over me. Why couldn't my father feel my pain and burst through the door to protect me as he had in the past when mother punished me for no reason?

"I don't remember much more about what went on or for that matter how long it lasted. I just remember my mother standing at the door once again, not saying a word but taking my hand and leading me back to the car. I wanted to tell her what happened, but I sensed she already knew.

"When we got home mother took me straight upstairs and prepared a bath for me. She took my pretty clothes which were now wrinkled and stained and put them in the laundry hamper. She never asked me anything about what happened after she left; she just carried on as though everything was okay.

"I soaked in the tub of hot water and wanted everything to go away. I wanted that day to have never happened. I wanted my mother, someone, just anyone to tell me that I would be alright, that everything was going to be okay, even though I knew in my heart it could never be. I just sat there in the bathtub as my tiny body trembled. The water was warm but inside I was cold, and the cold wanted to come out.

"I didn't cry anymore after that day and as best as I can remember, mother never took me back to that house, but she did take me to other homes and the same thing happened there. They were just different men with no expression to their faces. Most had the same calloused hands. I have since learned that they were hands that had seen a lot of hard work, coupled to arms that really didn't know how to embrace with sincere affection.

While too late to be of benefit, Yvonne's mother's condition has recently been defined as, Factitious Disorder by Proxy, a rare form of child abuse where a caregiver intentionally inflicts harm on a helpless dependent in order to gain perverted attention towards themselves. It is an appalling crime that can often turn deadly.

"Yvonne and I found a sense of normality by keeping ourselves active," Ralph would later explain. "We joined the local archery club where we established friendships with like-minded people in commonality. The fact that we each could send an arrow in the intended direction helped but wasn't a prerequisite.

"I did so well as to place second in the 1965 indoor Men's Free Style Expert B category with a score of 444. It is here that I came to know Art Williams, 'The Mad Archer of Ladysmith' fame."

While Ralph's free spirit seemed to suit Yvonne in their early years together, it proved to be his undoing before their seventh anniversary. "My living on the edge of what society considered lawful is who I was but it eventually rendered our lives together untenable.

"I worked at the Crofton docks as a crane operator where I offloaded the ships that came into port. One morning after a tiring nightshift, I came home to find Yvonne and our three children gone. So, too, was a large collection of their clothes, playthings, plus the car I had purchased for her. There was no note to say why she left or for how long, just that eerie silence that took over a vacant house."

There had been no precipitating argument leading up to the event nor any clear indication that she might have been unhappy. In retrospect, Ralph should have been able to recognize that the sheer number of unsavoury characters coming to the house for his product would have left Yvonne feeling uneasy.

"I sleepwalked through that nightmare, exhausted, stunned, angry, grief stricken and desperate for any ray of hope. After a few days had passed, I contacted her parents who by then had moved to Hope, B.C., but they stated they had heard nothing from her."

Months went by, followed by years and Ralph continued to hear nothing of his family's whereabouts. He fired off letters each week to her parents in hopes they would forward them on to Yvonne once she made contact.

He was confident she would not disconnect completely from every family member, so he held hope that at some point he could resolve whatever differences there might be between them. It never happened.

"I never forgot any of their birthdays or Christmas, with gifts passed along through her parents. I also sent monthly allotments of funds equal to what I believed would be child support, but my children continued to grow up without knowing me."

It has only been in this recent decade that Ralph's daughters reached out and reconnected, engaging with a man they never knew. Sadly, he was no longer in his prime, no longer able to offer them all he could muster, as he lived with heart issues and failing eyesight.

"While I was not blameless, I attribute the loss of these years to the insipid meddling of Yvonne's mother who, without remorse, did all she could to undermine our relationship.

"I retained hope for a number of years before I filed for divorce. Again, I was forced to submit the paperwork through her parents."

Ralph was certain they knew all along where she was but were unwilling to facilitate a reunion.

Eventually the paperwork came back signed, dated and void of any indication as to her place of residence. Where the paperwork had requested the reason for separation, Ralph had left it blank as he could think of none, but when it returned, Yvonne had printed neatly, irreconcilable differences.

"She could have noted any number of illegal activities I was involved in and appear as just one more abused wife, thereby selling me out, but she never did," Ralph acknowledged.

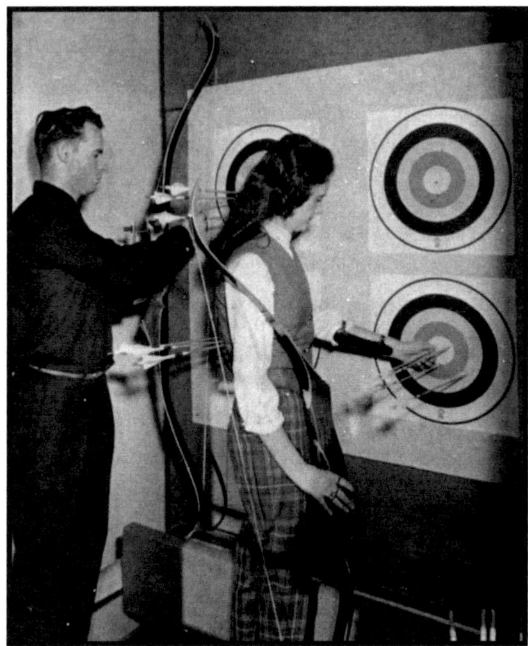

Ralph and Yvonne enjoyed archery.

Archery on the back of Williams' property.

CHAPTER 5

In 1968 Ralph met Kathy Schwabe at the party of a mutual friend. She was attractive and well-educated, holding a degree as a registered nurse and with a position in the Cowichan Valley Hospital in Duncan.

She entered the relationship with an adventurous spirit but Ralph never felt comfortable with sharing his entire past or for that matter his extracurricular vocation of production and distribution of weed. Still, comfortable in each other's company, they were married later that year.

As the years passed, they were blessed with two daughters, both of whom filled the void Ralph had endured since the day Yvonne ran off with his first litter. Binding them ever closer was the fact that both girls shared his passion for motorbikes, hunting and the great outdoors. Together, Kathy and he built a log home in rural Ladysmith, where they settled in for the long haul.

"It was a number of years before I introduced Kathy to my extracurricular activities. Rather than shock her in the direction of a divorce attorney, I brought only a few plants home at first. Those few grew into a few more until our entire front yard looked like a scene out of Jurassic Park with its exotic vegetation.

"Anyone who showed an unsolicited interest in my agriculture or any of the few individuals who considered themselves part of my inner circle, were kept at arm's length while I watched them like a hawk.

"To protect my family, I did all that I could to keep my clients away from our home. The underbelly of the industry does nothing to ensure a sense of well-being. Even so, some of the local bikers ignored my request and would show up at all hours of the day whether I was home or off tending my legit Longshoreman's job.

"Kathy was never comfortable with them when I was home let alone when I was away. It was common knowledge they had a harsh way of leveling the playing field if they perceived an imbalance. Besides, she had a professional career to protect. If word leaked to her superiors that she was entertaining members of the world's most feared criminal organization, it would, without question, jeopardize her good standing."

Inevitably, Ralph Ross Harris soon became a regular search name within the RCMP database.

There are numerous criminal databases in Canada. The Canadian Police Information Centre is likely the largest with over a hundred million queries annually, from 15,000 access points. It lists only criminal records, not intelligence files, hence Ralph Harris bypassed their resource for some time as it would have taken a conviction for his name to appear. For many years all his individual cases were stayed.

The RCMP are the next largest followed by ACIIS or the Automated Criminal Intelligence Information System. British Columbia had its own Organized Crime Agency in 1998 which was intended to target bikers and other forms of organized crime. But it only survived five years before it was absorbed by the RCMP's Integrated Organized Crime Unit. All the systems are victims of turf wars, belaboured by infighting, making them lethargic and overtly dysfunctional.

Kathy foresaw her husband's loyalties as being keenly misdirected with she and their girls clinging precariously to the proverbial ladder of his personal values.

Every siren that wailed off in the distance would cause her to stop breathing and wonder: *Was it going to turn into their personal driveway, resulting in yet another confrontation with the authorities?*

Kathy had learned from experience that if the cops were going to come after her husband, they would do so with as much stealth as possible and generally at an hour that reduced his options for an escape. With their lives together being interrupted so frequently, it was only a matter of time before Kathy gave Ralph his final notice.

On three occasions the cops raided Ralph and Kathy's home in pursuit of the grow-ops he insisted on having on their property.

"My only crime was the production of marijuana, but the prosecutor in each case was bent on proving that I was some mastermind behind a larger ring of conspirators, thus a member of organized crime," Ralph maintained.

Fortunately for Ralph, his first case was thrown out on a technicality, as were the second and third which followed. Each raid proved to be a complete waste of time, money, and energy. After the third set of charges fell by the wayside, he no longer had any doubt the cops had painted a bullseye on his back and they were going to do whatever it took to take him down. Nonetheless, he felt brazened by his victories and nothing was going to stand in his way.

Just the same, his growing notoriety injured Kathy's reputation at work and stressed all those who were swept up in the assaults.

On one occasion in 1988, a repairman working on the power line fronting Ralph and Kathy's home decided to trespass and inspect a secondary power pole on their property. In no time the worker found himself waist deep in one of the largest marijuana grow-ops on the Island and quite possibly the entire province at that time.

Being a model citizen, he immediately reported his findings to the RCMP. On this occasion, they not only hauled Ralph away, but Kathy along with her mother, who happened to be in the wrong place at the wrong time. The RCMP lacked the ability to discern who was innocent and who was not, so they bundled everyone up within reach and marched them all off.

Had Ralph's girls been older, the cops would likely have dragged them off as well. According to Ralph, "Most of the goons are reactionary by design, living by the principle of shooting first and asking questions later. As it was, they did wait long enough to permit my sister to come over and mind the girls before we were driven away."

By the following day, Kathy and her mother were released for lack of evidence. Ralph, however, remained in custody pending a bail hearing.

As Kathy predicted, her employer read of her arrest in the local paper and summoned her into the HR office where she was given a royal dressing down. The event didn't sit well so by the time she got home her countenance made it clear she had had less than a perfect day.

Fear of reprisal from Kathy's employer was not the sole cause of Ralph and Kathy's marriage falling apart. It was also Ralph's inability to keep his pants zipped up when not in his wife's company.

Kathy had known of his indiscretions for a number of years but chose to turn a blind eye for the sake of their girls. When, in 1988, their eldest daughter came home from school with her mother only inches behind, she was met by her father exercising his manhood on the master bed with a woman Kathy viewed as a close friend. Their daughter was horrified by the reality of what her mother had silently endured for so many years and to this day finds forgiveness evasive.

Ralph dominated Kathy's life and she hated him and loved him for it at the same time. She was constantly trying to break away and each time Ralph drew her effortlessly back.

Kathy sought help from those around her but they never bothered highlighting the kindness and strength that made her love him, only the cruelty and ruthlessness which made her despise him. Kathy knew Ralph was capable of destroying her if she let herself be run over by him. He was a dangerous man with a chip precariously perched on his shoulder. But therein lay most of his appeal.

One of their mutual friends approached Ralph and suggested he was not the only unfaithful one in the relationship as Kathy had been screwing around with the local dentist for some time. Ralph simply wasn't buying into the idea. "That is highly unlikely as it is so not Kathy. I am the guilty one here so let's not try and deflect the blame."

Ralph Harris in his front yard grow-op.

Ralph Harris.

Ralph with his family.

Ralph Harris with two of his girlfriends.

CHAPTER 6

Contrary to popular thinking," Ralph would say, "it wasn't my involvement in the drug trade that destroyed my marriage to Kathy as much as my inability to remain monogamous. I just couldn't resist chasing a pretty skirt if one crossed my path, which they seemed to do on a regular basis. As it is said about men in general, the small head can easily cloud the rational thinking of the one on their shoulders. For me, random sex with a consenting female is like a piece of metal being sucked towards a magnet. I was simply unable to resist their force."

Ralph enjoyed the challenge of bringing a beautiful woman to her knees. He especially reveled in those free-spirited girls who were unabashed about dropping their drawers on his first invitation. But the withdrawn ladies with their complicated personalities always seemed to offer the greater reward.

"Common sense never played a part in that aspect of my life. It wasn't until my daughter found me frolicking at home with a married woman, that I realized I had gone too far," Ralph conceded.

"As you would expect, my daughter went ballistic, then turned to her mother in an attempt to shelter her from the acid salt that would be added to her earlier wounds. It mattered not as Kathy knew the day would come. Just the same, she cooled down and gave me yet another chance.

"Moving product took priority over my lifc. Loyalty and appreciation for my wife and family remained firmly in second place. Rather than make every transaction myself, I had various people make thc runs in exchange for a healthy fee. Ray Ridges' girlfriend Krissy Murray was an eager participant until she developed paranoia surrounding her personal well-being."

Krissy offered another perspective. "It wasn't paranoia, it was real. I had been moving small amounts of whatever Ralph had to his paying customers until Ralph asked me to meet him in some God-forsaken part of the country for no explained reason. I had a feeling things weren't quite right so I asked Ray to look into it.

"Ray met with Ralph and reported back that Ralph felt I knew too much and had outlived my usefulness. In his opinion it was time for me to disappear. Ralph didn't listen to many people, but he did listen to Ray. Ray told him in no uncertain terms to leave me alone and thankfully he did. That was the end of my working relationship with Ralph," Krissy said.

Ralph Harris remembered a fateful day in 1990 that changed things for the drug dealer and his wife forever.

"Everything was running smoothly until January 23, when the cops fanned out across our property. I had been arrested an hour earlier for various charges under the Narcotic Control Act based on some informant stating I had sold him a few grams of cocaine.

"Without notice twenty cops showed up at our home advising Kathy that I had been arrested and they were there to conduct a thorough search of our home and property while the warrant would be arriving sometime later. As it was, the warrant never arrived at all that day and for that matter a copy was never provided to me or Kathy.

"A half dozen cops came in and spread throughout the house turning over every corner imaginable while others combed the yard with two dogs. Our youngest daughter needed to be fed and have her diapers changed, rendering me unable to monitor their activities while I tended to her," Kathy recalled. "They never appeared to be finding anything until I excused myself to the bathroom. When I returned the lead cop was holding a silver platter that he had removed from atop the fireplace mantle. I'm surprised he saw it as it was well above eye level. There on the platter sat two brown paper wraps which to me looked like the sheaths that held industrial razor blades.

"The cop asked me if I knew what they were, so I told him they looked like the wrappers from razor blades. He was quick to correct me by suggesting they were flaps of cocaine. Neither Ralph nor I used cocaine so I didn't know why they would be there. Having them show up as I left the room was suspicious at best.

"Other than this revelation, they found Ralph's secret hiding place in his bedroom dresser, his buried cache in the neighbouring backyard and the false wall in the shed, all of which held money, lots of money.

"The shed was where he met most of his friends (those I wouldn't allow in the house) and from it they retrieved a substantial amount of money. All in all they were in and about my home for close to six hours.

"The entire time the cops were here, cars would pull into our driveway, recognize the cop cars, and hightail it off down the road as quickly as they could. Much to their disadvantage, a single officer was stationed at the entrance to our driveway, for the sole purpose of recording each of their license plate numbers.

"Three days after the circus had left our property, I got a call letting me know my presence was requested at the Nanaimo station for fingerprinting and photographing. It was then I was advised they were going to charge me with the same offences as Ralph."

Ken Westlake represented Ralph while another lawyer, Mr. Martin, set up shop in Kathy's corner.

The cops figured they had Kathy centred in their crosshairs. It mattered not that the drugs were Ralph's, that the electronic scales, the score sheets, the unregistered firearm and the bucket load of cash had Ralph's fingerprints all over them. The home and property were registered in Kathy's name and hers alone. That made her responsible in the eyes of the law.

Without reading him his rights, Constable James Wakely of the Nanaimo Drug Section presented Ralph with the facts again and again while after each sentence Ralph would repeat "these issues have nothing to do with my wife."

"But you said you don't use coke, so that means the flaps and coke paraphernalia we found in your common bedroom must be hers. Look, tomorrow is Welfare Wednesday and all your distributors have been coming to your place looking to have their supply topped up. We already have two of your boys, John Hanney and John Takala, so we know the small amount of dope we found is not all you have," Wakely pressed.

"Your wife is in the health care business and if she gets charged with trafficking in cocaine, how is that going to play out when she goes back to work? You want your wife cleared so she can go home to your girls, and we want your dope. Can you figure out how this is going to work?"

Ralph wasn't ready to concede. "You say Kathy handed your boys two flaps of cocaine as soon as they started looking around, but that is not possible as she never knew where I hid it. There is no chance in hell she would have found it, plus she had no knowledge I was selling."

Wakely continued to push. "Look your wife is not stupid, she knows her husband. She's watched those degenerates coming and going from your shed for years and she's seen all that money lying around the house. How could she not know?

"There's a stash of coke on your property and we're so convinced of it that we're gonna dig the entire place up to find it," the cop threatened.

"What you got me with is all I have," Ralph retorted.

Wakely: "Then Kathy is going down. You're simply not being fair to your old lady."

Ralph: "Then I will show you where my stash is kept in the ground, but the two ounces you found is all I have."

Wakely: "Why is that?"

Ralph: "Because there's no coke around. There's no keys coming north at all. It's too hot down there. You know that. I know all about the dope, who's got it and who hasn't. The whole works. There is the odd flap out there, but that's all there is. It just hasn't been coming in since last July and you know that to be true."

Wakely: "What we do know is that Nanaimo is the first port it comes to and when it hits the rock it comes to you, then it filters down through God knows how many hands before it reaches the street.

"Where in heaven's name did you get all those thousand dollar bills?"

Ralph: "How did you find that hole?"

Wakely: "The dog went nuts when he smelled the marijuana. You shouldn't put your money where your dope is."

Ralph: "Well, if I admit to what you have and a few other things, will you leave my old lady alone? She's got nothing to do with it. She doesn't do drugs. She doesn't even smoke."

Wakely: "Ralph, you got a stash hidden somewhere and we want it. You're not going to convince us that the two flaps we popped you with is all you have. We know you've been selling. Takala, Ingram, Darwin and four others have all bought from you this past week, so we know you have a stash somewhere. We also know that when we popped John Hanney yesterday, he was on his way over to buy the two ounces we have you with. Welfare Wednesday is the most productive time of the month for you, so we know you've got a stash somewhere.

"We also know there is a shipment coming in and we know it's for you. Are you going to trade it for the love of your life, for your two girls and their piece of mind? Kathy is going to go to bed crying tonight, not because you are in jail, but because she has worked so hard to build up her reputation in the hospital. You're painting her into a corner and to date she is sticking with you for better or for worse. By your actions, you are telling her, 'There is only one person in this world that matters and that's me.' If your daughters were eighteen, they would be charged as well.

"Is that unregistered, illegal side-arm Kathy's as well?"

Ralph's only thought was how are the ballistics to that piece going to come back to bite me?

It was 9:23 p.m. Six hours of grilling had passed without a break and the cop had finally worn Ralph down to the point where he agreed to lead them to the stash buried on his father's property next door. He did this on the understanding that nothing would happen to Kathy or his parents as each were unaware of him using their land for such purposes.

Within the hour, Kathy was released. The fact that they had no evidence to support their charging her was purely incidental to the decision.

While in confinement Ralph learned that a mid-level distributor whom he had supplied for years decided to save his own hide by ratting him out as his only source. What this fellow failed to consider was that Ralph doesn't take kindly to rats and that he's known to have a long memory.

Ralph elected a trial by Provincial Court Judge which proved to his benefit as the judge acquitted him stating she was "critical of the conduct of the police, finding that various searches, including the search of Kathy's home in which $125,000 in Canadian currency was seized" were illegal. All the resultant evidence, therefore, inclusive of real evidence, was ruled inadmissible."

RCMP Sgt. John Abbott was not prepared to leave the matter there but passed the RCMP findings regarding the large sum of money on to Brad Anderson of the Special Enforcement Branch of Revenue Canada. Anderson immediately printed out Harris' income and assets and concluded Harris "had a great deal more assets than his payroll from the Crofton Mill would support."

In December 1990 and again the next month, Anderson contacted Harris with a request to discuss tax matters, listing eight requirements to provide information by the deadline of June 26, 1991. Harris ignored the request which led to charges being heard by Justice Maughan, who after hearing all the evidence entered a stay on July 9, 1993.

"Information provided to Anderson would not have been discovered save through the breaches of Mr. Harris' Charter of Rights and Freedoms. Hence the RCMP exercised flagrant disregard for Harris' rights," Justice Maughan determined.

She also ruled: "It is an abuse of process to allow one arm of government to rely on evidence gathered by another branch of the same government.

"Revenue Canada's actions would never have seen the light of day had it not been for the illegally obtained evidence within the preceding case and Sgt. Abbott's attempt to gain a conviction by utilizing a back door to circumvent the state's breach of the accused Charter of Rights. It was a flagrant abuse of process."

The crown appealed Maughan's decision to the Supreme Court of B.C. who in turn upheld the lower court's ruling.

The matter of Ralph's infidelity, followed by Kathy's arrest and ill-feelings at work, brought Kathy to the point where things had to change and clearly they were not going to change unless she made change happen. Kathy showed Ralph the door with the understanding that he could visit anytime to participate in their daughter's lives.

One affair led to another with Ralph and in no time he found having only one woman on the hook at a time insufficient to hold his attention.

"I got to a point where I had a number of women on the go simultaneously. Many of them knew of each other but gave no indication they minded sharing. By locker room standards, I was endowed well beyond that of the average male and to the point where it was my belief the women found it novel or entertaining."

One of his most frequent conquests remarked, "He was a real charmer. He was playing the field with a number of local women at the same time but most of us knew we were not his only prospect. For us, it just didn't seem to matter.

"He was so big he would have had to drain every ounce of blood from his brain to get it all the way up so it was a good thing he couldn't, as he would have caused me some serious damage," the woman offered candidly.

"My indiscretions eventually overshadowed Kathy's life," Ralph confesses, "and may have contributed to her final breaking point. She was patient in so many ways but basic pride would not allow her to continually turn a blind eye to my behaviour. For the record, I never stopped loving her. These other relationships I had were not based on love, they were just sexual encounters that stroked my oversized ego.

"For the good of our girls, there was no running quarrel on the surface which they could see. Kathy was very good about addressing my social activities behind closed doors and with a temperate voice she made it perfectly clear that I had the morality of an urban gutter rat."

Unlike many stay-at-home wives, Kathy had always been an independent woman with a mind of her own, plus a professional career in which she exercised her independence daily. There was no way in which she could continually switch her decisiveness off at the end of her hospital shift.

By their twenty-second anniversary Kathy had insisted that Ralph move out of the home they shared, leaving her and the girls to enjoy a degree of peace, quiet and predictability.

Ralph found himself on the street looking for an alternate form of shelter, while Kathy assumed the primary role of raising their girls. Unlike the situation with his first wife, Kathy never deprived him of access to their daughters, for which he remained eternally grateful.

Moments like this are defining. Life can never go back to where it once was. That simply never happens. Some men learn from the experience. Most feel something, while for others, it changes them forever as they try to adjust to a new way of life.

Looking for a place to call home, Ralph found a very private twelve-acre parcel of land a short distance north of Kathy's property on Rosalie Road. He moved a small trailer onto it as a temporary shelter while he built a new home.

The design was based on a Cape Cod style with 3,174 square feet on two levels, four bedrooms and three baths, offering far more creature comforts than the one he had shared with Kathy all those years.

"Unlike the log home I shared with Kathy, this one was well insulated."

Included within the project was an oversized two-story barn that provided space for a well-equipped workshop on the main level, a highly sophisticated hydroponics grow-op at the rear of the main level and throughout the upper level. Those outdoor grows which depended on the weather to produce a saleable crop continued but were no longer paramount to his success. From that day forward, every aspect of the plants growing cycle would be monitored and controlled to provide ideal production quotas. "My pot business took off. I had interbred the best seeds from the four corners of the globe with the best we had locally. It took me a few years, but patience eventually paid off. I was producing the best bud known to man and the industry soon recognized that to be the case.

"Rather than play the risk associated with trafficking, I left most of the market to the bikers with their established network. They had a standing order for all I could produce and within no time I was netting $20,000 a week on the pot alone. Couple that with my other products and I was cruising on easy street."

Wishing to ensure a defensive posture, he installed a motion sensor on the gate at the top of his long driveway to alert him of any unscheduled visit. This, at the very least, offered a few seconds to run or hide that which he didn't want the cops to see.

Life returned to normal until 1997 when an unnamed informant persuaded the RCMP to take a look at the grow-op springing forth behind Ralph's barn.

Within a day, Cpl. Dan Kingston of the Ladysmith Detachment sequestered the RCMP helicopter so he could complete an aerial surveillance of the subject property while taking photographs of the home and surroundings to support his expert testimony.

"With a warrant in hand, Kingston knocked on my door and insisted I join him while he walked about my property. The outcome was predictable, following which I was arrested and driven to the Ladysmith detachment.

"As a norm, my plants were ripped from their pots and tossed into the back of a waiting truck, representing a huge financial loss for me. A few plants were held as evidence while the others mysteriously disappeared. I would never be one to suggest the cops kept the weed for their personal use, but a few of them did appear happier than normal in the days that followed."

You would think the cops would eventually figure out how to do their job, but that doesn't seem to have been the case. Once again, the charges were dropped after the judge declared the search invalid and the evidence inadmissible.

Ralph and Kathy's home - shed to the right.

Ralph and Kathy's home.

Ralph's shed.

The inside of Ralph's shed.

Some of the cash seized at Kathy and Ralph's home.

Waterproof container where Ralph hid his stash.

CHAPTER 7

In December of 1999, Ralph Harris's good friend Art Williams vanished off the face of the earth. Facing a trial for having been the engineer behind the largest synthetic drug cartel of its day, he was flying his small Cessna back to the Nanaimo airport after a meeting with his Vancouver criminal defence lawyer.

Prior to his disappearance, Art had often found himself on the front page of most daily newspapers as he continued to frustrate the law with his production and distribution of MDA, often referred to as the love drug.

While Ralph was never able to dial himself into the production taking place in Art's world, he did represent a large segment of the distribution network.

At precisely 9:15 on the evening of November 30, 1977, Art Williams' plane dropped from the Vancouver's traffic control monitor as though it had taken a nosedive into the waters off the Tsawwassen ferry terminal. While some debris consistent with his plane was found, no substantial component or his physical body was ever recovered, leaving his disappearance a mystery that remains until this day. In the opinion of the U.S. Coast Guard captain who attended the search: "Had I known there was so little to be recovered, I would never have bothered participating."

E Division, the RCMP's control centre for Vancouver Island Organized Crime, found that deep breath they had been longing for. While the loss of any life causes a measurable dent in a family, the loss of Art Williams represented the end of a decade long struggle to cut the head off the dragon of the syndicate that manufactured and distributed MDA up and down the West Coast of North America to epidemic proportions.

To them, the disappearance or death of Art Williams would immediately result in the flow of this particular social drug being stemmed. Or had it?

Ralph Harris recognized the vacuum brought about by Art's absence and not wishing to see someone else jump into that void he scurried over to Art's Westdowne Road lab in Ladysmith and secured all the equipment and supplies remaining on his property.

With the help of a chemist friend, John Bertram Waller, they leased a rundown home in Nanoose Bay, some 38 minutes or 48 kilometres from Ralph's residence in Ladysmith. Before the week had passed, they had stockpiled all the chemicals they needed, from the same suppliers that had fed Williams for so many years and in turn were pumping out MDA which the authorities deemed "had a chemical signature similar to Art Williams and his partner Dale Elliott, yet slightly different."

The RCMP were beside themselves. They had spent millions of dollars and thousands of man hours attempting to bring Williams and his inner circle to justice, only to have that sweet taste of victory slip through their fingers shortly after Art vanished.

Feeling somewhat gratified that they had at least cut the legs out from under Williams' enterprise, they were dumbfounded when the drug once again flowed freely into the streets.

Sharon Hitchen was a frequent user of MDA in those days.

"I found it gave me a feeling of euphoria and a love for everything. Whatever I was doing, whether standing in a slow-moving river in the middle of nowhere looking up at the sky, playing with a small fluffy kitten in the grass or talking to an ancient man with a cane sitting alone on a park bench, it was always deep and meaningful. I had this peaceful, calming and introspective feeling if left to my own devices.

"The downside to MDA was that during my trips, I was willing to give away anything I had in my possession, including what money I had, any food in my backpack, the favorite neat rock I kept in my pocket or my own personal stash of MDA, so they could experience what I was experiencing on that day."

For his part, Ralph Harris was also savouring the delights that were coming his way through the so-called love drug.

"I felt the world was my oyster," Harris explained. "With two elements of the drug trade tied up and little to no competition, life was good, the flow of money was even better. I was now pulling $20K a week from my grow-op and my share of the proceeds from the MDA at $3.25 a capsule was triple that."

Ralph's wallet grew fatter and fatter with each passing day. He never trusted banks if for no other reason than they would question where such large deposits came from. No matter what his explanation, they were obligated to report all large deposits to the feds. He was so flush with cash that he ended up burying it in his backyard in coffee tins, munitions cans and other watertight containers.

"He had this rock which formed part of the exterior to my mother's house that he would pull out leaving a large void he could stuff money into," states one of his daughters.

"As ludicrous as it may sound, there were times when I was unable to remember all the spots around the property where it was hidden," Ralph confessed. "I'm confident the day will come when some future owner will be planting tulips and hit their own personal Lotto Max."

Ralph could have tried to launder the money but felt he would still have difficulty explaining away the large quantities of cash on a Longshoreman's salary. "I wasn't making much more than $20,000 a year so it wouldn't take a genius to figure something was amok. Either way I would have to put my trust in a third party. Such individuals glean anywhere from 15 to 18 per cent off the top and would then try to screw me out of my life savings or turn crown witness to save their own hide when faced with a judicial hiccup.

"I was dealing on both sides of the border, leaving me with as much Canadian currency as U.S. to deal with. Getting caught on the Canadian side of the border would get me two years less a day if I was convicted of laundering, but if my luck failed me on U.S. soil, I would see sixteen years in a federal penitentiary with no access to Kathy and the kids. On a lighter side, I guess that proves crime still pays in Canada."

Ralph needed a constant source of adventure that would take him out beyond the edge of sanity.

"Once the lab had become routine, that exciting edge I had reached for seemed to fade away."

Never one to settle for what's working, the day came when he convinced his chemist to shut down their production of MDA in favor of the latest and greatest. With the coming of the 1990s and the rave scene, MDA had lost its flavour with the youth as the taste of the day morphed into its second cousin, Ecstasy or Molly (MDMA).

Like MDA, it is a product of a German pharmaceutical company dating back to 1912, originally intended as a parent compound to synthesize medication to control bleeding. During the Cold War era, the U.S. Army and the CIA experimented with the drug, code named 'EA-1475' as a psychological weapon. Therapists referred to the drug as 'Adam' because it returned patients to a more innocent state and made them willing to communicate and participate in the psychotherapy process.

It achieved the desired effects which included altered sensations, increased energy, empathy as well as basic pleasure. When taken orally its effects begin within 30 to 45 minutes and will last up to six hours.

At the time, the feds saw no concern with its potential for abuse and therefore no reason to ban it, until it started flooding the streets as the party drug of choice in 1985. Even so, the ban allowed its use in the 1990s to treat those suffering from PTSD, anxiety within autistic adults and patients with terminal illness.

Ralph Harris found the demand for Ecstasy ramped up higher among the youthful generation than its predecessor, especially on weekends when parties were going down. Hence, his profits with the MDA paled in comparison to sheer volume associated with its cousin.

For the local authorities, Ecstasy snuck into the area quietly. "It arrived in small bags brought by friends to share at secretive, insular clubs around the city. It was nothing big, just something that like-minded friends would pass among themselves while dancing away the weekends," reports a RCMP spokesman. "We didn't even know it was here as it never showed up as a 911 drug. Parents would drop their kids off at clubs thinking everything was okay because they didn't serve alcohol.

"But the secrets could not be contained. It was sort of a New Age hippie thing; very cool, very mellow, no problems. Then it just started to grow. Students from the university were popping it to mellow out during a particular class. It was, like, everybody was doing it. Word of the raves spread, as did a new drug scene that started sweeping the city."

With everything running like clockwork, Ralph was approached by the Nanaimo bikers' club President Zeke Mickle asking if Ralph knew of a place where they could set up a lab to manufacture Speed, a drug that worked somewhat like Ecstasy in stimulating the nervous system, but it had that extra hook where unlike Ecstasy, it was addictive.

As a white, odorless, bitter-tasting powder, it dissolved easily in water or alcohol. Considered to have a high potential for abuse, it was none-the-less legally available in the United States through prescription to treat ADHD or attention deficit hyperactivity disorder and obesity. It can be smoked, snorted, injected, or taken orally. While the rush will last at best fifteen minutes, a mass section of the drug crazed population stood in line for its arrival. As a close cousin to Crystal Meth, it has since risen to prominence.

With his Ecstasy lab busted, Ralph Harris needed but a millisecond to accept the invitation. He extended the offer to his friend Mike Orr and Phil Stirling, as he knew one or both of them would know of a location that would work.

As it turned out, Phil's buddy had a farm in the area of 100 Mile House that was secluded enough to allow such a setup, yet not draw a whole lot of attention. Approximately six hours north of Vancouver, the place had supported a large grow-op that had flowed beneath the cops' radar for a number of years. According to Phil, the owner was open to diversity, but better yet, the guy was heading overseas for a spell and preferred not to leave the place vacant.

The rent was high enough to suggest he didn't care what they did as long as he got his rent on the first of each month. Furthermore, he was quite happy to be kept in the dark.

After the deal with the landowner was struck, Ralph learned he was not going to play an active role in the day-to-day operation. He was relegated to set it all up, for which Zeke promised to pay him $2 million as a silent partner. This turned out to be one more of those occasions where a profound difference exists between making a promise and delivering on it. Zeke never intended to keep his word or pay anyone down the line, including the homeowner's rent.

Fool me once, shame on you. Fool me twice, shame on me. When it came to Zeke, Ralph would never be led down that garden path a second time.

RCMP evidence of MDA/MDNA lab.

Nanoose lab.

Nanoose lab.

Nanoose lab.

Ralph's lab equipment.

Storage in Ralph's lab.

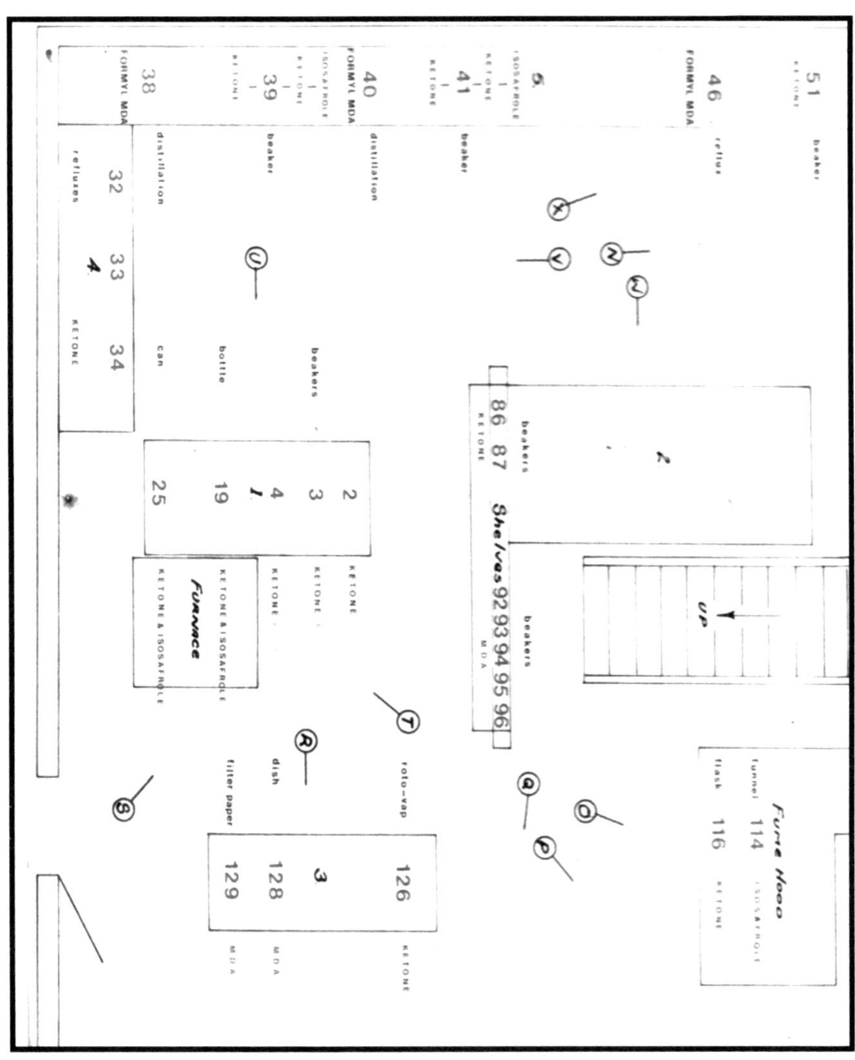

RCMP evidence of MDA/MDMA lab.

CHAPTER 8

Ralph Harris's friend Art Williams, had provided well for his wife in anticipation that one day he would not be around. The Ladysmith property on which Margaret lived was transferred into her name so the rent from the adjoining duplex would go straight to her, plus he gave her a large sum of cash for her safekeeping.

Margaret placed approximately $60,000 of the money in an ice-cream bucket that she hid in the woodpile next to her cabin entrance. This she used for her day-to-day needs. She took the balance of $90,000, stuffed it in a watertight munitions can and hung it on a rope down a hand dug well behind her cabin so it would not be a carrot to those who wished to deprive her of it, yet it remained easily accessible should the need arise.

Ralph was a regular visitor to Margaret's place, so he knew the windfall had to be eating a hole in her pocket. By nature, she was a money hungry woman, so this played well into Ralph's endeavours.

"Margaret and I had spent many an evening together after Art disappeared. Rumors were floating around that I was doing drugs while having an affair with her but unlike the other women in my life she could never be more than a friend."

She was one of the few who knew how Ralph made his money and he was confident he could trust her in the same manner Art had done for so many years.

In the 1980s cocaine was just starting to surface as the drug of choice and it seemed anyone who was someone in the social world was using it. It had a retail price on the streets of Vancouver of $32,000 a kilo and somewhat higher in the more remote towns and villages of the province. When the Hells Angels sat down with the Quebec mob in the 1990s, they jointly agreed to fix the price at $50,000 a kilo. Even in the 1980s it didn't take an Einstein to calculate that risk versus profit favoured getting involved in its importing.

Early in 1979, Ralph threw Margaret a proposal. If she would match his investment in a substantial buy of Colombian cocaine he would arrange the shipment and distribution while they would equally share in the profits. Margaret was all over the idea and without hesitation pulled the $90,000 out of the well and handed it to Ralph.

There are only two ways to bring dope in from South America, by air or by water. It mattered not if you were flying or sailing it into Canada, there are three basic components to such a plan. First is the acquisition and delivery of the product to your ship or plane in proximity of South America, followed by others aiding in its transportation to your desired destination, which could be as simple as a rural runway or offloading onto a second boat close to your home port, likely during the dark of night. The final step is the unloading and moving the cargo into a storage facility, giving enough time to facilitate distribution. Again, others must be involved in the risky business. Each step opens you up to those wishing to gain favour by ratting you out to the cops, while each step also eats into the desired profit.

The key to success is keeping the final destination and the name of your buyer secret from those who provide the dope. This is a dog-eat-dog business, and the provider would just as soon remove you as the middleman from the equation if it meant more profit for them. The pilots of the aircraft or ship also need to remain ignorant as to who is loading their craft and with what. At times, ignorance can truly be bliss. All dealings must remain on a need-to-know basis. The only information required is the course of travel, the ultimate destination, expected time of arrival and their port of call on return. Once again, those who unload the cargo should know nothing until the last minute. This reduces any chance of a loose tongue during a drinking binge. When the success of the mission is assured, those responsible for unloading will be advised where and when to show up to perform their job, not a minute earlier. This protects the entire operation and each individual along the food chain.

In the weeks that followed their decision to work together, Ralph and Margaret both drove south of the border and then flew the rest of the way to make arrangements for pickup and delivery. Margaret had a clear understanding that once the product left Colombia there were no guarantees. Ralph, in turn, made it clear to her that if the shipment went sideways it was their shared loss.

It was common knowledge that the bikers had infiltrated the largest union controlling British Columbia's shipping ports, the International Longshore and Warehouse Union (ILWU). In doing so they managed to fill many of the key positions granting them unfettered control over what came and left via commercial shipping, whether it was from the Roberts Bank Superport in Delta, South Vancouver, or the Surrey docks. By this means, the bikers dominated the flow of cocaine into the Pacific Northwest and the export of the infamous B.C. bud, the latter of which had provided Ralph's livelihood since his youth.

As a Longshoreman for over 40 years, Ralph was qualified to make an intelligent assessment of the situation at the port. "The last word I received suggested ten full-patched bikers, plus thirty of their associates held ILWU cards, with some being 25-year veterans. A few held administrative positions within the union, while others worked as dock administrators where they could place containers and manpower wherever they wanted. The majority had their feet on the ground as load coordinators, crane operators, forklift drivers and as the last link to the chain, transport drivers who delivered the containers to their rightful owners."

When nosy workers or uninvited visitors asked leading questions, they were told in the most intimidating way possible: "Don't interfere with port business. Cargo can fall, people can lose their balance and drop into ships' holds. Accidents on the waterfront are just written off as accidents." The bottom line is the port authorities are fully aware of what's going on and don't care.

For decades the ports were monitored by the Canadian Port's Police, where intelligence was gathered and investigations initiated.

The three primary Vancouver ports represent the largest point of entry for trade goods in Canada, averaging $29 billion annually from ninety nations. It sees cars, electronic goods, food supplies and drugs roll across the same tarmac wharf.

Mike Toddington oversaw the Vancouver Port's Police as Chief of Security during the early 1990s. It didn't take him long to recognize things were amiss on the docks and in the offices of its administration, so he began to raise concern as key positions within the port authority were compromised by individuals who had close ties with the bikers.

When the cousin of a patched member assumed the position of receptionist for the Vancouver Ports chairman Ron Longstaffe, Toddington passed along his written concern over the ease she had access to sensitive and confidential information. But it fell on deaf ears.

Toddington and his force decided to open their own investigation which they referred to as "Project Eh". They followed the woman from her office each evening to a home in Burnaby, which the RCMP had been monitoring as a possible crack house. The Ports Police took swabs from the door handles of her Volkswagen Beetle and from her driver's license, both of which recorded high, positive readings of cocaine.

On January 17, 1997, Toddington paid Norman Stark, the former Ports police chief and now the port manager, a visit. Stark offered, "We know she has relatives who are involved in organized crime. You've got a problem, as she is a serious risk." In his opinion, it was a matter for the personnel administrator and that if Toddington or he were to make an issue of it, the woman would likely move forward with a case of harassment.

On March 4, Toddington got a call from Sid Peckford, his superior officer and was told, "Just write it off and leave it at that." Toddington indicated he wasn't prepared to do that. Fifteen days later Toddington was fired.

Toddington had raised so much concern while insisting on action by his superiors, the Port Police were disbanded in July 1997. Simply put, they were not good for business.

Prior to the Ports Police being disbanded, over $1.25 billion in drugs had been seized but that amount represented a small fraction of what was being offloaded on the west coast of B.C. Within hours of the Ports Police office being vacated, all the investigative work completed by Toddington and his crew, inclusive of intelligence reports, and confidential police files, vanished.

Toddington received an unofficial call from a colleague in Ottawa stating they were suffering the same fate. "They were destroying material they knew they shouldn't be destroying; three drawers worth of intelligence involving more than seven thousand people who had worked for the Port Authority going back ten years. Their findings were that 75 per cent of those under study had criminal records. One drawer was packed with active files." All those records were now ribbons of paper in the bin under the shredder

With the cops no longer on the ground, tailgate parties around the wharf continued unabated. Small shipments of drugs were tagged along with bona fide cargo. When these dual-purpose containers arrived, they were moved to a less conspicuous location on the dock where small trucks could back up to the container, tailgate to tailgate. The seal would be broken, and the desired contents offloaded without interdiction. Taped to the inside of the container door or the package of contraband would be a fresh set of seals which are then affixed to the container as it made its way back into the mainstream of the dock and onward to its declared destination.

"When importing contraband, it only makes sense to employ the bikers as an insurance policy and have the load shipped through the Vancouver ports with minimal risk of interception," Ralph explained. Canadian customs inspectors are only able to check three per cent of the million plus containers that enter Canadian ports each year. It becomes a simple shell game played out by the chosen few on the docks who ensure containers are moved about like peas so they are inaccessible to the inspectors, thereby guaranteeing the flow of drugs will continue unabated.

Ralph Harris was counting on this system working seamlessly to deliver his and Margaret's shipment.

"Club members are the first people who access the ships when they come into port and they have the handling of sensitive cargo down to a science. These boys would have my container flagged well before it entered Canadian waters. They would know its exact size, the colour of the exterior, what company name was stenciled to the side, the serial number stamped on it, plus, exactly where it sat in the hold of the ship.

"When it came to offloading, the boys would make certain it was buried deep enough amongst the other containers on the dock that the feds would never be able to inspect it. When land transport was arranged to Vancouver Island, the boys would ensure no inquisitive eyes were roaming about the docks while they loaded it onto my contract semi. Following that point in time, I was on my own.

"Even though the club happened to be my end client, they still received a percentage of its estimated value as a handling fee, so everyone would go away happy."

But as luck would have it, the bikers informed Ralph that his and Margaret's container never made it to Vancouver. It was either seized or lost en route as the ship made its way north along the coast of California. Containers often fall from ships in rough waters but that was just too coincidental for Ralph's liking.

He dug as deep as he could but was unable to determine if someone had sold them out or if it was just a lucky bust on the part of U.S. Drug Enforcement. They will never know the answer to that question, but there went Margaret and Ralph's bankroll.

To say she was unhappy would be an understatement. What mutual trust there had been between the two evaporated in a blink of an eye. By her estimation Ralph had received the load, sold it and stiffed her, keeping all the proceeds for himself. Nothing he could say was going to convince her otherwise.

"Everyone who has dealt with me knows I am a straight shooter. I would never screw someone who I have an agreement with as trustworthy business relationships are hard to come by," Ralph maintained.

Margaret refused to buy into Ralph's story and threatened to share all she knew about him to the feds if he didn't come up with her share of the profits by the end of the week. He had no doubt she meant what she said, leaving him with one option.

It didn't matter whether someone was a friend or not, if they seriously threatened Ralph or anyone he cared about and refused to back down despite a concerted amount of encouragement, he would ensure they never had a chance to carry out their threat. Innocent looking as Margaret was, she was no exception.

On the evening of March 4, 1979, Ralph paid her one more visit, crossing his fingers, hoping she had reconsidered her position. But that was not the case. As soon as he stepped over the threshold of her cottage door, she lit into him. Ralph had anticipated this and prearranged with Ray Ridge and his brother Dave, both of whom Ralph trusted with his life, to park nearby at 10 p.m. and remain there for an hour. If Ralph didn't show up, they were to get on with whatever else they had planned.

At approximately 9:30 p.m. Ralph convinced Margaret to go out for a drink and see if there was some means by which they could move beyond the impasse. Surprisingly she agreed and threw her cape over her shoulders, leaving her purse and everything else on the kitchen table. He figured she would have been suspicious and refuse to go anywhere with him. But street smarts were not her forte. As she soon learned, that oversight would be her last.

Ralph told her they would head 25 minutes south of her place to a well-known pub in Duncan but first he had to pick up a buddy en route. As planned, the Ridge boys, Dave and Ray, were sitting on the side of the highway exactly where he had directed. Ray climbed into the passenger door of Ralph's truck, wedging Margaret in the middle, while the other followed in his own car. There was no love between the Ridge boys and Margaret as she found them both to be offensive, while they in turn considered her arrogant and belittling. It was the perfect marriage for what was to follow.

They drove to Dave Ridge's house on Sahtlam Road in north Duncan with the excuse he had to pick up his wallet which he stated he left on his dresser. When they arrived, he asked if they wanted to see the well he had dug beside his workshop and as though it was all choreographed, Margaret ambled along behind. He explained how he had dug the well by hand and had eventually given up after hitting bedrock sixteen feet below the surface with no sign of water.

As natural curiosity drove Margaret to lean over and look down the hole, Ray popped a single slug into the back of her head and over she toppled, clean as a whistle, all the way to the bottom. She was only 56 years of age when her life ended.

"Ray was one of my most trusted friends, but he had a tendency to get things twisted from time to time," Ralph would later say. Even though his health was failing from Hep C, he held up his end of the agreement as the three grabbed spades and threw a few feet of soil on top of her body, just to bury it from any unwanted eyes. They then drove to the Duncan pub in hopes of washing her image from their minds.

"One day later, the cops offered Ray $750,000 if he would rat me out. He had no money at the time so it must have been tempting, but he wouldn't do it. That's the kind of guy he was. Straight up and always there beside me no matter what turn the event takes.

"Shirley Ferguson and her boys were still living in the duplex beside Margaret's cottage so there was no way of hiding from her the fact that I was there the night Margaret disappeared, but I put the fear of God so deep into her heart that I knew she would never talk. Besides that, the dumb cops never even bothered to question her."

As it turned out, the investigating officer who interviewed Margaret's family in Alberta, told them, "She had been murdered by the bikers and that if they were to create a fuss, their own lives would also be in jeopardy."

Hence, for the last 45 years, they have lived in fear of uttering a single word regarding Margaret's demise.

They had purposely left the well on Dave Ridge's property open, as the bikers told Ralph they would have a couple more bodies to dispose of in the next day or two. True to their word they showed up the following night with the remains of someone Ralph recognized and another guy he didn't. To close that chapter in their lives, all involved pitched in to fill the well back up to the surface.

It was only a few years later that Dave Ridge was found in his Chemainus home with what was reported to be a self-inflicted wound to his head. It was suggested by the authorities that he had become distraught after having problems with his girlfriend and took his own life. But not everyone bought into that notion. Some of those close to him felt he may have been the victim of a different form of relationship that turned sour.

For years Dave had filled his off-hours as an expert gunsmith. He could take fully automatic weapons that had been rendered inoperative and bring them back to life for those who had need of a firearm. Most of his clients suffered from some form of paranoia and those same people seldom found comfort in loose ends, even if the victim was their sole source of hard-to-find weapons.

According to a close friend of Margaret's, "Margaret was a nice lady who never swore. She would do a little pot and after you got to know her, she would attempt to be the centre of attention. She had been in Art's shadow for so long that once he was gone, she was determined to be in the spotlight. She had a mind of her own and could be real bossy or outspoken if she felt like it. For some strange reason her personality morphed 180 degrees with the disappearance of her husband. She took on more of a masculine role. Dressing in Art's clothes she figured she was smart enough to take over the drug trade where Art had left off."

Ralph Harris suggests Margaret was in over her head in that world. "She never had the moxie or the quick wittedness to make those key decisions that were needed in a deal."

While she and Art had been separated since the early sixties, she remained loyal to him and held the belief he would return one day so they could live out their senior years together. Unfortunately for her, that never happened.

Looking back, Ralph made a few errors that fateful night. The first was parking his truck on Margaret's property where anyone driving by could see it and secondly using a well to dump her remains, one that was freshly dug and under the scrutiny of a number of people who frequented Dave Ridge's property. Lastly, it was a known fact that Ralph was one of only a couple of people who knew how to access Margaret's property without raising a ruckus from her dog Flipper and the geese that had free run of the land.

Over the years people started speculating as to why the well was filled in so quickly after her disappearance. Putting two and two together, those that knew Margaret and the whereabouts of the well concluded that it was her final resting place. That suggestion was made to the RCMP but the Mounties expressed no interest in excavating it. With today's DNA testing, it's for certain some discarded gum wrapper, cigarette butt or soiled clothing would make those involved prime candidates for a life sentence.

Fortunately for Ralph, the cop assigned to Margaret's disappearance was considered ill-equipped. His peers suggested his training was insufficient to take on an investigation of this nature. According to the RCMP's public relations unit, the detective spent close to two years interviewing everyone associated with Margaret but his list did not include Ralph Harris, the Ridge boys or Margaret's tenant who resided fifty feet from her cottage. Regardless, everyone who had seen Ralph's truck in her yard that night chose to keep their mouths shut.

One of the three fellows who had been involved, had his wife visit Margaret earlier the same evening on the pretense of purchasing her golf clubs. The lady was given explicit instructions as to when she should arrive, how she was to get past the geese and dog, what she was to say to Margaret and the precise time she was to leave. She, too, was never interviewed by the cops.

"When I arrived, Margaret asked me if I wanted a cup of tea, but she was visibly nervous about something. I believe my husband could kill someone if he felt it necessary, but he never told me he had been involved in her disappearance, while he did make it quite clear that he had been a bystander to at least three murders," the woman recalled years later.

The police investigator did nothing for the typical 48 hours stating they were dealing with the case as a missing person. Along with the majority of his peers, he relied on the notion that Art had simply returned from the dead in the middle of the night and picked her up so they would spend their final years together in a warmer climate. As charming as that thought might have been, it was far from the truth and only blinded the investigator's view of what was a more obvious solution.

Rumors of Margaret's disappearance were as numerous as there are people to propagate them. Many attached themselves to the novel idea that Art did in fact return to scoop her up to join him during their senior years. Others figured she had wandered up into the hills behind her home and suffered a heart attack, yet others pointed a finger at the reigning president of the local bikers who was stiffed by Margaret after he agreed to fall some timber on her South Wellington property. Fortunately for Ralph, this same fellow had shot off his mouth a few days after her disappearance, claiming that he had whacked some old lady, no name or reason given. Ralph's silence allowed each theory to gain momentum and add yet another layer of confusion to what actually happened.

On February 5, 2009 the location of Margaret's remains and possibly three others, were reported to RCMP Chief Superintendent Randy Wilson of E-Division in Victoria. On that occasion his underling, Staff Sergeant Ray

Carfenton, responded, "While the file is still active, there is no interest in pursuing this information unless a signed confession is presented from one of the individuals who were involved in her demise."

As the sole means of providing closure to the family of Margaret Williams, the owners of the property upon which the well is located were contacted and an agreement was given to enter onto their land for the purpose of exhuming her remains.

Professor Brenda Clark of the Archeology/Anthropology Department for Camosun College in Victoria was employed to bring four of her graduate students to the subject property where a thorough forensic examination of the well would be completed.

The plan was to move slowly down through the layers of fill looking for any evidence such as chewing gum, cigarette butts, tissue, soiled clothing or the murder weapon. With the acquisition of such evidence today, the identity of the perpetrators could be revealed through DNA testing, a technology that was not available at the time of Margaret's disappearance.

The location of the evidence would be documented, photographed, and secured in accordance with sound forensic practices all under the supervision of retired Staff Sgt. Dave Staples and Scotty Gardiner, the retired Chief Superintendent of E-Division. Both had volunteered to oversee the operation.

The latter two men would act as expert witnesses to the work so that it stayed within the guidelines defined by standard police procedures. Brenda Clark brought to the table Professor Mark Skinner of the Simon Fraser University along with the best equipped secure forensic lab in British Columbia.

The entire operation would be financed by private money, therefore costing the RCMP or Canadian taxpayers nothing.

During the week preceding the commencement of work, Staples and Gardiner paid Ray Carfenton one last visit in an attempt to gain RCMP support. As a result of that meeting, Staples was told, "The file is still open, but if he or anyone else disturbs human remains while executing the work, he and the remainder of the crew would be charged with tampering with evidence." The two men came away disappointed. "The RCMP's work ethics have changed so much from the time we were on the force," Staples lamented.

Fearful of reprisal, Dave and Scotty backed away from their involvement and recommended that all others involved do the same. The following day, with no explanation, the owners of the property retracted their invitation to access their land.

To this day, no effort has been made to retrieve the remains of Margaret and possibly two others.

Art Williams had always declared he had a journal in which he recorded every dealing he had with Ralph Harris, the bikers, and his entire inner circle, suggesting that if any one of them betrayed him, he would blow the whole thing wide open, and they would all go down together.

With both Art and Margaret out of the way, Ralph was determined to make certain that journal never fell into the wrong hands. He and Ray Ridge spent days pulling the walls apart in Art's lab, Margaret's cottage, and the vacant duplex, plus all the outbuildings, searching for the journal without success. With no alternative, they torched everything. If there was a journal, it would have to rise from the ashes before it would trouble them.

"We had no trouble getting the lab and Margaret's house to light up, but the duplex seemed to defy the laws of nature. With the sky aglow from the fires and sirens wailing in the distance, we abandoned the duplex and crossed our fingers the journal wasn't there," Ralph, the erstwhile arsonist recalled.

CHAPTER 9

David Giles, a high-ranking Ontario biker, contacted Ralph Harris in November 2000. More commonly known as Gyrator, he offered to exchange a suitcase full of cash for a few tons of Colombian cocaine. The only glitch seemed to be that Ralph had no personal contact within the South American cartels. He did, however, know someone who was well connected.

Forty-six-year-old John Philip Stirling had been introduced to Ralph in the early 1990s through their mutual friend Mike Orr, or Mikey as he prefers. Phil and Mikey became friends while they were doing a stretch in William Head Penitentiary for drug deals that went wrong. Unlike Phil, Mikey received an additional two years for smuggling grenades and rocket launchers into the area. His attitude was, 'Go big or go home'.

Forever attired in his grey Stanfield, Phil remains to this day a strapping man who better fits the image of a burly long-haul driver than a sophisticated international smuggler. Standing at six-foot-one and carrying a formidable 260 lbs, he doesn't stand out in a crowd with his brown hair and eyes. His features are so ordinary he can vanish into a busy setting in the blink of an eye.

Unlike Ralph, Phil's primary source of income since his youth had not been cultivating pot but importing it. Phil's profits were not based on the premium B.C. bud that Ralph engineered, but rather the second rate marijuana that flowed north from Mexico. Even so, the ready market for the lesser quality product had put food on his family's table for years.

While consumers knew the Canadians had the best weed in the world, it was simply a matter of price point and demand.

Phil Stirling began smuggling as a kid by moving a pound across the U.S. border in the pockets of his jacket. This graduated to ten pounds stuffed in his luggage, followed by a hundred pounds which required a wee bit more thought when it came to transport.

"In those early days there were no scanners at the airports, no drug dogs and no Customs agents that concerned themselves with importation. In the truest sense, it was an open border," Stirling explains.

On occasion Phil would supplement a pot deal by bringing in a small amount of cocaine. As awareness rose of what he and others were doing, methods of concealment changed. Hidden panels within luggage became the roots of the era of sophistication.

"Now the Colombians are making lawn chairs out of cocaine. It looks and feels like a lawn chair, it passes the smell test and will even support a realistic weight. But rendering it back into a snortable powder is time consuming and not for your average importer," commented Stirling, drawing from his vast experience in the business.

Phil Stirling and Ralph Harris were considered by many to have the perfect marriage. Stirling offered a 96 per cent success rate in smuggling, plus he also brought to the table all the Colombian/Mexican connections an importer could ask for. More importantly, he was a man who could thread a ship of any size through the eye of a needle and not scratch an inch of the painted hull.

Harris, on the other hand, had never been convicted while it was common knowledge he maintained a finger on the pulse of every biker and mob boss that mattered north of the U.S./Canada border. Finding a single individual who had both groups in their Rolodex was unheard of. Having a working partnership as well-endowed as theirs was highly unusual.

Phil and Ralph had never worked together but Ralph knew it was the route he had to go if a deal with the bikers was going to materialize.

"I introduced the idea to Phil in an odd but effective way. I knew where he lived in Metchosin just outside Victoria, so I drove down Island and caught him as he was walking up his driveway. Without saying a word, I handed him a brown paper bag containing ten stacks each containing $10,000, then without a word I turned and left. I let a month or two pass and the brown bag never found its way back to me. So I figured he had either decided to work with me or at least I felt I could consider him to be on some form of retainer.

"When Gyrator came for his next visit, we made a second unannounced visit to Stirling, but this time at a cabin he rented each summer on Cowichan Lake. Lea Sheppe from the Nanaimo Club and another guy I only knew as Joe tagged along for support. Dumber than a load of bricks, these two came fully decked in their colours.

"Can you imagine showing up at a discrete meeting and a couple of goons show up wearing their colours. It's as dumb as the Aryan Nation pounding the Confederate flag into the front yard of their covert headquarters. To me that was the height of stupidity, but what can I say."

Phil's family was milling about on the lakefront when the men arrived, so they all piled into his boat and headed out into the middle of the lake where their hushed conversation was less likely to be picked up by those who had no need to hear what was being talked about.

The root of the conversation was Gyrator wanting to know if Phil had received the hundred grand, whether he was happy with it, and lastly if he would attend a meeting with a few of his peers in a couple of hours.

Gyrator left with the Nanaimo bikers at this point while Ralph remained at the cabin with his girlfriend Joanne Tossin.

The scheduled meeting took place at Ma Miller's Pub, adjacent to the Goldstream Park on the outskirts of Victoria. Phil and Ralph were the first to arrive, which may have been by Gyrator's design to never be too careful.

One of the new guys looked more like a banker than a biker as he walked in with a laptop tucked under his arm. This should have been one of those high-water marks in Ralph's career which would have set him up well for retirement, but much to Ralph's disgust, Lea Sheppe motioned for him to move outside for a brief chat and this is where the two remained for the duration of the meeting while a further club member held down the adjacent table with his back to the wall so he could monitor the movements of the other patrons.

"If you've ever had an issue with the cops," Ralph would say, "they won't tail you longer than six months. If they find nothing worthy of laying charges, they are generally reassigned to mess with someone else's life. At this point in time I had been clean for the better part of a year, so I don't know why there was an issue between the club and me.

"When I was having issues there were seldom less than twenty guys assigned to monitor my every move and sometimes up to fifty. A pigtail of that size is pretty easy to pick out."

"We became pretty adept at shaking a tail," Phil agreed during a later conversation. "But no one is perfect. Unlike some guys who don't have a wife and family – or for that matter a fixed address – all the cops have to do is stake out our homes. Common sense rules that we will return sooner or later. Once they see us pull into our driveways, the cops just pick up where they left off."

Ralph Harris knew the code and he followed it faithfully, as do outlaw bikers.

"I'd never spoken to my wife Kathy while we were together, or any of our mutual friends about what I do. Besides the fact she never wanted to know as she was confident it would have been unhealthy for her and our girls.

"The bikers are really secretive about their activities and look poorly on those who are dialed in for no justifiable reason. As it is, the cops have made Kathy's life miserable enough. If she knows nothing, she can't inadvertently say something to complicate my life."

Phil told Ralph later that the banker had made it clear that he was in control. Hence he had maintained the flow of conversation at the Ma Miller meeting. When he opened his computer, Google Earth was displayed outlining his thoughts on a proposed route and pickup coordinates.

He wanted to know how long it would take to sail from Victoria to Colombia, then pick up a load and return. He pointed out that whatever timeframe Phil chose, it would be fixed and unmoveable. Ralph and Phil would be paid $100,000 up front, plus they would be reimbursed for all their hard costs like fuel, en route maintenance to the ship, port fees and whatever else came up. Lastly, he wanted to know how the duo intended to conceal two tons of coke in whatever ship they chose.

Phil outlined his demands to the bikers. "I don't have a ship at this time, but the hundred grand will help in acquiring one. As for hard costs, any ship I acquire will need its engine serviced and the tanks filled before departure. This alone could run as high as $70,000."

The deal was struck. Within two hours, Phil had nailed down three workable rendezvous points along the Colombian coast where a pickup could be made, plus a couple of exit routes if things went bad.

At the close of the meeting, Phil told Ralph that he had been forced to swear that he would tell no one of the arrangements, including him. Ralph was royally ticked as he saw this as an attempt to cut him from the deal. All Phil could say was, "It will be fine. The thing is still going ahead," plus he promised he would not shut Ralph out of the conversations in the future.

Ralph was hardly in a place to walk, as Phil's knowledge of the cartel's home ports and their country's coastline was imperative to the success of any endeavour.

Paranoid as hell during the forty-minute drive back to the lake that the cops may have been monitoring their meeting, Phil trained his side mirror on the traffic behind, asking Harris more than once to pull off so he could see if someone was tailing them.

CHAPTER 10

In the months preceding the trip to Colombia, RCMP Constable Todd Preston gained information from an unnamed source that Ralph Harris had once again been unlawfully producing a controlled substance, to wit: cannabis marijuana, contrary to Section 7(1) of the Controlled Drugs and Substances Act.

Checking the RCMP database, Preston noted that Ralph's residence had been searched as recently as 1997 resulting in the seizure and destruction of marijuana plants, yet no convictions were entered. Ralph Ross Harris continued to operate freely.

Preston prepared a request for a warrant based on the principle that, "There are reasonable grounds to believe that there is a controlled substance or precursor, contained or concealed on the related property."

His request was supported by an aerial inspection of the property at 1,400 feet elevation, on September 17, where it was noted "three rows of large plants were seen to the rear of the barn-like structure. These plants were consistent in shape, colour and texture to that of marijuana."

After confirming the existence of the plants once again by air on September 21, Justice Leo A.T. Nimsick signed a warrant to search the property known as 2949/2955 Rosalie Road in Ladysmith, with specific exclusion of all structures and outbuildings.

The owner of the subject property was confirmed to be Ralph Ross Harris.

At precisely 9:15 on the morning of September 23, just three months prior to the scheduled sailing of Ralph and Phil, a search warrant was executed. In the company of a number of officers. Sgt. Sean Bourrie of the North Island Drug Section, knocked on the front door of Ralph's home and presented him with a formal letter on RCMP stationery, identified as File #2000-193 and a copy of the warrant outlining the purpose of their visit.

Ralph was handcuffed by Cpl. McLellan, read his rights, which he acknowledged as understanding. McLellan then asked Harris to show them the interior of his home for "reasons of officer safety."

Harris told him, that with the exception of himself, the house was empty, but he cooperated just the same. With the home cleared and locked up, Harris was walked approximately 150 yards up the driveway to the area surrounding the barn.

Const. Preston confirmed the existence of the outdoor grow-op, which included twenty-two mature plants. At 9:25 Ralph shocked the cops by volunteering, "My outdoor plants are all mouldy and garbage, but I've got lots indoors."

At 9:30 a.m., the garage doors were opened overpowering everyone within range by the strong odour. To the hum of commercial fans, Preston viewed an extensive indoor grow operation. He ceased his investigation and rendered the structure secure pending acquisition of a second warrant that would be more inclusive of the buildings.

Const. McKenzie transported Ralph to the Ladysmith detachment where he consented to having his fingerprints taken and image photographed, after which he was placed in a cell. As he was processed and issued prisoner number 66, he handed a prepared list of medical requirements to the clerk highlighting prescription needs which would address his high blood pressure and Type 1 diabetes. The list included syringes and medications, Altace 5mg, Hydrochlorothiazide 25mg, Metoprotol 25mg, Plavix 25mg, Lipitor 10mg, Humalog and Humulin N.

At 10 a.m., Const. Preston returned to the Ladysmith detachment where he applied to Justice Nimsick for a second search warrant embracing the barn. This he received at 12 p.m. The investigation of Ralph's property was then turned over to Const. Weihs.

Const. Weihs noted, "The barn contained three rooms. One-half of the main level supported a three-stage indoor growing operation where small, cloned starter plants sat beneath fluorescent lamps. The second half of the main level was a workshop. The clones were short in height but in a healthy condition.

"The upper level or third room, contained additional plants two to three feet in height, beneath high intensity discharge lights. All plants were potted in soil and serviced by an automated watering and nutrient system."

The RCMP estimated the street value of that which they seized to be in the range of $120,000 to $152,000. At 1:42 p.m., holding only a warrant to search the barn, Const. Weihs entered and searched the residence of Ralph Harris.

Ralph was released after signing a promise to attend the March 1, 2005 preliminary hearing.

Albert King agreed to represent Ralph at his preliminary hearing and for the duration of his trial, subject to receiving a retainer of $2,000.

Regina v. Harris commenced at the Duncan courthouse 9:30 a.m. sharp on November 4, 2005.

The Crown was seeking a nine-month sentence along with a substantial fine, plus the forfeiture of any and all firearms he may have, a curfew, and abstinence from alcohol, drugs, along with regular urinalysis, plus permission for the RCMP to enter his property at any time without notice.

As with every preceding case against Ralph, the judge ruled the evidence inadmissible due to the improper means in which it was gained. Many of the officers involved were veterans with 15 to 20 years under their belt. Ralph could only shake his head as to how unable they were to meet the requirements of standard law. He snickered at how he had foiled their attempt.

"I found that if I start telling them everything they could hope to hear from the moment they confront me, they inadvertently enter the evidence without reading me my rights or having the proper warrants being in place. This was the case of them accessing my house and my barn without a proper warrant after I volunteered information about its contents. In each of my many cases, they fell victim to their own incompetence."

CHAPTER 11

Prior to Phil Stirling setting sail for Colombia, he was forced into a confrontation with two Mainland cops. The pair had approached him in an unmarked car as he was exiting a Victoria mall.

The passenger of the unmarked car lowered his window and instructed Phil to get in the back. Phil with his usual bravado replied, "Why would I want to do that when my mother taught me never to talk to strangers and you two look about as strange as they get." The request didn't end there as the guy behind the wheel responded, "Get in or go to jail, your choice."

Not knowing what they had on him, he felt he had no choice but to cooperate. The fellow in the passenger seat turned halfway and introduced himself as Pat Convey, head of RCMP Organized Crime Division for the Lower Mainland. He then introduced the driver as his partner Dave Watt.

There was a period of silence before Convey continued. "Phil, don't ever lie to us or I will put your sorry ass in jail for the rest of your life. Do you understand? We know that one or more of the Hells Angels is going to ask you to captain a ship to Colombia to bring cocaine back and we want you to cooperate with us."

Phil was stunned as he and Ralph had only been approached by the bikers a few days prior. He was dumbfounded as to how these two cops could get wind of the offer in such a short period of time. Convey acknowledged Phil's quandary, handed him his card, and suggested he think it over.

In Pat Convey's opinion the deal on the table was a good one for both sides. "There was no downside. Stirling would lead us to the buyers, then to the distributors, while our team would work their way up the ladder to the money. If it went as planned, Stirling and his family would not have to testify, but slip off into the night under the witness protection program to some warm and friendly climate."

Phil made no attempt to follow up with Convey or his partner. Tired of waiting for a reply, Convey decided to press the matter.

He demanded a second meeting in another Victoria underground parkade. This time he cut to the chase. "What do you want to do? We know from our Montreal contacts that something is happening."

Thinking on his feet, Phil figured that they didn't know as much as they were letting on. They made no mention of Harris and his involvement. Had they known about the $100,000 he already had, their demands would have made mention of that as well.

Phil attempted to call Convey's bluff. "I want a million dollars, you have to buy all my assets at fair value, including my home and companies, plus I want $10,000 a month for the rest of my life, in addition to a $10,000,000 policy with my wife the beneficiary, on the chance I come to some untimely end."

"Is that all?" was Convey's only reply, laced with an air of sarcasm.

"You asked. The ball is now in your court." Phil opened that back door of the car, got out and walked away without looking back.

A few days later Convey asked for yet another meeting in the same parkade. Based on a conversation he had with their mutual friend Mikey, Phil concluded Ralph had already been rolled. To reinforce that thought in Phil's mind, Convey only seemed to know what Ralph would have known having been excluded from the bulk of the meeting at Ma Miller's Pub. When they met again, Convey enquired about information that would fill in those gaps. In Phil's view, his assumption on Ralph being turned held merit, even though he lacked certainty.

Phil gave them very little at that second meeting. He says he gave the cops no names, but only the descriptions of all the players. "It was useless information as Convey and his partner clearly knew more than they let on well before my deal with the bikers had been locked up," Phil says.

"Without Ralph, I met the bikers at a Ladner bar to discuss the trip. Convey and his buddy had arrived well enough in advance to position themselves a few tables away. Ralph didn't know about the meeting, so there went my theory on him as the rat."

Convey later told Phil he was going to have to wear a wire when attending further meetings, to which he replied in no uncertain terms that such a move would ensure his death along with his wife and son. Disgusted, Phil left the meeting without further comment, while flipping them the bird over his shoulder.

The following morning Phil drove to Ralph's place in Ladysmith, met him in the garage and enlightened him as to how the whole venture had gone south. He was confident he had been followed to Ralph's and that under the circumstances, they should abort the venture. Ralph agreed without hesitation.

By that time, Phil was seeing cops hiding behind every bush at every corner. Before he left, Ralph's girlfriend Joanne arrived, so Phil cut the discussion short, telling him to think about it.

The following day Ralph took the matter to Lea Sheppe of the Nanaimo chapter, to which the biker replied it wasn't their concern as the cops had been paid off. "Don't stop anything, get the boat together and act normal."

Ralph drove to Phil's place in Metchosin, but regardless of what he said, Phil refused to have any part of the deal.

"He slammed the $10,000 down on his kitchen table and told me I could take it back. While I supported his feelings, I refused to pick up the money. To do so would have gotten me killed, along with Phil.

"From that day forward, we figured we were forced into the trip not only by the cops, but the bikers as well. Whatever happened was going to be on the bikers' heads," Ralph explained.

While Ralph and Phil were dealing with Gyrator, he in turn was working on behalf of the Russian mob operating out of eastern Canada. Therefore, indirectly, Ralph and Phil were working for the mob. Everyone knew they were not a group of men you wanted to drop the ball on. This was no longer a matter of dealing with the devil, but with all his imps as well.

Years later, Pat Convey offered his take on the situation: "These types of events are like an eclipse – they don't come every year. You have to take advantage of them when they do and you have to respond."

So the boys on the ground wasted no time in giving Phil's demands the green light only to have it scuttled sometime later and without explanation by the upper echelons of the RCMP.

"After I told Phil our deal was off, he instructed me he was going to head south regardless to go fishing. Realizing this was nothing more than a ruse, Phil told me he had been threatened via email on the ship's computer, leaving him with no option but to move forward with the mob's deal."

CHAPTER 12

It was quite by chance that Phil garnered his connections south of the border. Spread over seventeen years and involving over fifty trips north with tons of Mexican weed, he came to know a bona fide doctor in Sinaloa, Mexico.

As is often the Mexican way, this doctor was getting it on with the mistress of a major cartel drug lord. It seems the mistress was ticked when the cartel leader refused to leave his wife, so out of spite she gave all the guy's connections to the good doctor, who in turn gave them to Phil, upon receipt of a small donation towards his retirement fund. This gave Phil access to a number of names of potential suppliers, associates and other key individuals.

As part of the joint venture, Phil found an ad in a boating magazine for the *MV Western Wind*, a 109-foot, steel-hulled fish boat, with a capacity of 137 ton and a top cruising speed of 13 knots. It was being promoted as a bank sale.

"At first glance she was a little rough with her stained paint flaking off the hull and a two-inch-wide hole running six inches along one side. There was a simple solution for the paint, but the hole penetrated not only the outer skin of the ship, but also the interior fuel tank." Phil scoured every other possible source for a ship but found none.

By sheer luck, Phil knew the former owner as a fellow fisherman who had worked the B.C. coast out of Ladner. He had fallen on hard times with the illness of a child and the Royal Bank of Canada foreclosed and listed the ship as a distress sale for $225,000.

The ship had seen better days, but it would hold 10,000 gallons of fuel, sufficient for two months at sea. Phil's friend Mike told him the engines were cheap on fuel, easy to maintain, and appeared to be in better shape than the rest of the ship. With a little digging Phil found they had recently been rebuilt, along with most everything in the engine room. Add a few months' work, plus $40,000 and she could be brought back to life. And, of course, $5,000 to repair the hole in her side and tank.

The wheelhouse sported all the latest equipment from multiple SSB radios, plotters and GPS. All were brand new and almost everything worked perfectly. "Fortunately for us," Ralph added, "the bank had never troubled itself to have the ship surveyed or for that matter even given it a cursory once over. They had absolutely no clue of what they were selling."

The difference between the asking price and what the boys had to spend would require some expert bartering or very creative financing. Negotiations with the bank began with a chilling tale of how the hole in the ship's side and tank had been leaking fuel throughout the marina for some time, leaving the duo surprised that the bank had not already received a call from Fisheries or Environment Canada.

Phil applied continued pressure by explaining the ship would need a 'Steamship Inspection', since it was a commercial vessel and the repairs were likely insurmountable when coupled with the asking price. At the close of his rant, he offered $100,000, which he indicated was more than generous under the circumstances.

Following a period of silence, the banker offered to finance the difference, but the boys declined. Phil suggested there were other ships worthy of consideration with a lot fewer headaches, even though this was a blatant lie. The banker expressed regret that his offer was just too low to satisfy those who had the final say but he would present it just the same.

Somewhat deflated, Phil showed pure genius. Knowing the bank needed a little push, he called a friend at the marina, who knew a friend in the Coast Guard, who in turn filed a report with the Ministry of Fisheries, stating the *MV Western Wind* was leaking fuel from a ruptured tank into the Fraser River.

The following morning the banker called Phil and asked if he would consider $135,000, but Phil stuck with their original offer, repeating the key points of their earlier story. The banker never mentioned having received a call from the Coast Guard or Fisheries but hesitated only a few moments and accepted the $100,000.

By the end of the day Phil had transferred the club's $100,000 into the bank's account and minutes later she became theirs. Phil and Ralph's quest for the pending coke shipment, having a street value of $330 million, was one step closer to reality. With an eager buyer for the shipment already in place, the venture was a no-brainer. Financially, that is.

Unlike most ship christenings where a bottle of champagne is smashed against the bow, the partners christened the *MV Western Wind* with a cup of strong coffee and a fat rolled joint.

By the time Ralph arrived at the Ladner marina, Phil had already commissioned Shawn Cochrane, an engineer friend, to get the ship ready for sail. Phil swore Shawn could tear an engine down in his sleep and put it back together before breakfast, with no spare parts. "You can't run any ship, of any size, without a good engineer on board."

He rounded out their crew with John Corbin of Chase, B.C., a cook who went by the name of Red, plus a young lad who, in hindsight, should never have been involved. The combination of skills each member brought to the task were impressive.

"Having any less than four men on board a good-sized ship would be ludicrous. These guys are rock solid, so I was prepared to stake my life on them," Phil said.

None were told the true nature of the maiden voyage other than it was a fishing trip for which, depending on the catch, they would be paid well. On fish boats, it was the practice that the crew shared financially in the success and the failure.

Ralph stands by his initial decision. "If you want to pull off a deal of any magnitude, you want to do it with someone like Phil. He has no fear of interdiction, nor of doing the time if required and if lethal force is the only option, like me, he has never proven squeamish."

Phil Stirling was no stranger to the inside of a jail as his first conviction in 1989 netted him five years for bringing a substantial amount of cocaine into Canada. Inside, he was a model prisoner, so he did only eighteen months. Such leniency is typical of the Canadian judicial system.

"You need to recognize up front that the boys in blue and a number of the upper bureaucrats don't really want to stifle the flow of drugs north of the border," claims Stirling. "They all benefit financially one way or another."

The RCMP and city police justify their annual budget increases by the need to curtail organized crime. In 2021 forty-six per cent of the Canadian RCMP budget was directed at organized crime, but not at the arrest of those involved, rather it was steered towards money laundering. What they managed to seize, they added to their budget as income. Likewise, the lawyers and the court system would suffer a great financial loss if the unregulated flow of drugs was legalized overnight.

There was another occasion when Phil was a guest of a Florence, Colorado prison for trafficking in coke. While he may seem unlucky at first glance, he continues to hold a success rate well in excess of 90 per cent. Not many smugglers can boast of such numbers.

It was in prison that Phil met Javier Guzman, a cousin to Joaquin Archivaido Guzman, also known as El Chapo. This chance meeting led to Phil spending a week as a guest at the notorious El Chapo's residence. Phil's Mexican conduit would remain firmly in place. El Chapo is currently serving a life sentence in a Colorado prison.

With everything coming together, Phil and Ralph left the ship in search of a truckload of essentials: mops, brooms, cleaning fluids, enough food to last them a couple of months, plus a dozen donuts to keep the crew happy over the short term.

Ralph directed the supplies from the truck to the ship's storage while Phil went straight to the engine room to oversee Shawn and a buddy changing the fuel filters and preparing the engine for its initial start-up.

Unlike a car engine, these mammoth diesels are no simple matter to fire. They first require a compressor which is operated by an auxiliary engine. It needs to build 600 pounds of air pressure to drive the pistons in the ship's main engine down at a force that will ignite the diesel fuel and, if lucky, the engine will run perfectly.

The auxiliary started up without an issue but it took Shawn fifteen minutes to build up the pressure needed to turn the main engine over. The starter was not your typical button or switch, but rather a long lever on the front of the main engine. When the air pressure was sufficient, he slammed it down sharply and the main engine sprung to life, with no unwanted smoke and no issues. "She ran like a baby. A noisy one at that, but that is normal for a diesel," says Phil.

Even with all the first-class equipment in the wheelhouse, he figured he needed a new VHF and antenna, plus an updated mapping system coupled to a navigation computer. These two items would be essential to make such a long voyage. The ones on the ship were slow to respond and at times they did not even respond.

First thing the following morning, Phil paid the marine electronics store down the road a visit. He had worked with the Asian owner several times and knew from past experience the Chinese don't talk about anything they see or hear.

The owner of the shop followed Phil back to the ship where he gave the entire electrical system a once over. Having sat for so long, most of the wire connections were corroded from the salt air and needed a thorough cleaning, while other pieces of equipment had been jerry-rigged together by the previous owners. Mr. Chang made it clear he would not leave until everything was in good working order. Ralph and Phil considered the $2,000 cost to work his magic was money well spent.

Their next stop was a shop that repacks life rafts. Rafts have to be unravelled, cleaned, checked for leaks and then repacked at least once a year. The inspection date on the *Western Wind*'s raft had expired two years earlier. Being an eight-man raft, that task would set them back another $2,000.

Never wanting to be too far from the club's money, Gyrator showed up at the ship with the banker in tow and hauled Phil off to a nearby restaurant. "I like the boat," the banker said. Before Phil could comment, the banker leaned in and asked, "how long are you going to be before you are ready to leave? I have to make arrangement for a specific time of your return and once that is done, I cannot change the date, so please don't make any mistakes." Phil has never been one to speak without thinking so he took a minute to ponder the question. He knew an incorrect answer may cost him his life. "We will be ready to leave Victoria on New Year's Eve."

Having seen Ralph on the boat when they arrived, the banker continued, "You have already been told that Ralph was not to come close to this operation and yet there he is on board. We want him gone, now." Not seeing any option but to cooperate, Phil told them he didn't need Ralph's help any longer, but "I would appreciate you telling him because I don't want any hard feelings. I have enough to worry about." The banker agreed to break the news.

Before they separated, the banker slipped Phil an envelope that contained three email addresses for his personal use. He requested that he be emailed with an update on November 25, using the first number. It seems the banker would be in Colombia on the 25th, so if he didn't respond, Phil was not to go anywhere until they connected.

"While I was working on the *Western Wind*, the day Phil met with the banker," Ralph remembered with disdain, "Gyrator called me as their meeting ended and made it clear that I was to leave the ship immediately and get my ass as far from the ship as possible. It was not a request. If I failed to react as instructed, they would walk away from the deal and while they didn't say as much, I was confident they would mess me up pretty good to offset the inconvenience I had caused. By reputation, Gyrator was not a man to be toyed with. It was the banker's feelings that my current scrutiny by the RCMP was such that if I was seen in or about the ship, the venture would be jinxed from the get-go."

Under silent protest, Ralph committed to involve himself in the ship's logistics upon its return. This left Phil to do all the heavy lifting both ways between Canada and Colombia.

With 1,000 gallons of fuel on board, Phil set off for Victoria's Point Hope Shipyards in early December of 2000. There, the hole in the hull would be patched and the entire ship repainted inside and out.

The Shipyards would also rework the propeller shaft, rudder, and steering system to reduce any vibration or sonic noise to a minimum, this being a must when fishing tuna. The final bill rang in at roughly $25,000.

While out of the water the *Western Wind* faced a CSI style inspection by a Coast Guard inspector. This is a mandatory requirement for every commercial vessel at least once every four years, leaving the owners entirely at the inspector's mercy when it comes to the list of whatever they deem necessary. They make you pull the thruster shaft clear out of the hull as well as all through-hull fittings so they can ensure all are safe and seaworthy. On occasion, they will insist on a complete hull x-ray to see if there is any metal fatigue or rot. The inspector they were stuck with was well known for putting many of Phil's peers out of business by his ridiculous demands. Departmental rules also dictate that all work, inclusive of the removal of a single bolt, must be completed by the shipyard's staff.

The lesson in this story is: don't buy a large ship unless you have deep pockets, or you can be assured of a large paycheque within a short period of time.

As it was, the ship had sat in the Fraser River for who knows how long. With the Fraser at the marina being mostly fresh water, the effects of salt on the ship were minimal. The zinc bars affixed to the hull were only 50 per cent consumed and the sixteen through-hull fittings appeared excellent with little to no damage. As the inspector handed Phil his list, he knew he had dodged a serious bullet as it included little to nothing of concern.

One day while the ship was dry-docked, the banker showed up at the Hope Point gate dressed in his banker attire complete with his fedora hat. As soon as Phil acknowledged him, he made his way next door to the Princess Mary Restaurant, with Phil in pursuit. The banker was looking for confirmation that the New Year's departure was still realistic. Phil made it known that he had not left the shipyard since the vessel arrived and would remain there pushing the work forward until the ship was underway.

Phil explained what work was being completed, including the Coast Guard's list and again that it would be completed as agreed by New Year's Eve. The banker asked how their money was holding up to which Phil responded, "well". The banker didn't look, behave, or speak like the other bikers but at the same time Phil knew frivolous questions from him were not welcome. Business with him would continue on a need-to-know basis and it was agreed that they would meet for lunch each day at the Mary, just at different times. The banker would show his face at the gate and that would be Phil's invitation to attend.

CHAPTER 13

Everything went better at the shipyard than Phil had expected, allowing them to set sail three days prior to Christmas. The banker hung around long enough to see the ship lowered back into the water, then take on fuel and supplies one last time before it powered out under the Johnson Street Bridge toward the open water.

In all cases, a wise man in this line of work assumed his phone was tapped, so it was agreed that the ship and all its crew would run silent from the moment it sailed, to the point of their return, unless things went terribly wrong. As Ralph Harris would say, "No news is good news." When they had to communicate it would be via coded messages on a single sideband radio which provided a range of over 1,000 miles.

It wasn't until the *Western Wind* was 2,400 miles southwest of Cabo San Lucas, Mexico that Phil broke the news to his crew about the trip's true intent. Their cargo would prove to be the largest volume of cocaine ever seen on the west coast of North America.

"Shawn Cochrane already knew the basis for the trip but if any of the others wanted to jump ship, I made it known they were free to do so, no hard feelings and definitely no reprisal. For their troubles, they would be given $20,000 and their flight home from Cabo," Phil explained. Surprisingly, the entire crew agreed and signed on. Phil guaranteed each of them $1 million which would come from the sale of his and Ralph's 20 per cent share of the load.

"While Shawn knew more than the others, even he didn't know all aspects of what was happening. I always had the practice of ensuring those who deliver and load would not know the final destination or who the actual end buyers were. Plus, my crew would have no idea who paid the wages of those who brought us the product. They only knew their course and they never found out what our final port of destination was until I had made my own mind up which was not more than a day or two before we made land. No person or group of people knew anything more than they absolutely needed to know to perform their job. This protected the operation to some degree from rats. It also insulated the individuals further up the ladder from arrest and conviction."

The following day, the crew started removing the 140 bolts that held the ship's inner side panels in place. These would expose the twin 5,000-gallon fuel tanks on either side of the ship. There was enough room behind these panels to store the cocaine out of sight for the trip home. Each fuel tank could devour three small bedrooms end to end.

En route, Phil had received the emailed coordinates for the rendezvous point from the Columbians, being 200 miles due west of the Ecuadorian and Colombian border.

"The Colombians have never been a group of men to arrive early or show up at all for that matter, so I had no choice but to patiently jockey with the tide. At a half hour before sunset, the sky was cloudless and the seas were moving steady with the ebb of the tide, while a 20-knot wind pushed against our starboard quarter."

In time the ship's radar registered a small fishing boat broaching the horizon twelve miles northeast, on a direct course from Bonaventura, Colombia.

"The ship slowly closed the gap between us and then hovered four miles off causing us to look like two gladiators trying to size the other up."

The radio had been silent, the wind had stopped, and the sun was just setting and the crew was tense. Phil had no way of knowing if they were friendly or if they were pirates leaving just enough time to distribute the guns and Molotov cocktails to his crew.

Channel 16 on the VHF is known around the globe as the mariner's emergency channel. Every Coast Guard monitors it twenty-four hours a day, as did every sea-going vessel no matter its home port. Just the same, someone bellowed over channel 16 in broken English, "Hey Amigo, ready to work?" Phil nearly crapped his pants. You can be assured the U.S. Coast Guard heard that communication, so Phil responded, "Ola Amigo, Cambio tu fucking radio, por favor, rapido 27." It took two tries before the dimwitted Colombians figured it out, after which they made straight for the *Western Wind*. Had I had an ounce of brains, I should have aborted the trip right then and there.

"It turned out to be a small fishing boat, maybe sixty feet in length, with no flag. They had what appeared to be a thirty-man crew, with the captain leaning out of the upper wheelhouse window. Our smaller crew had already deployed our large Scotchman buoys and were standing by with lines so the two ships didn't slam into each other."

Once tethered to the side of the *Western Wind,* a couple dozen unkempt Colombians formed a human conveyor belt hauling 25 kilo bales of pure cocaine from their boat's hold, across their deck and up onto the *Western Wind*. It was nothing more than mindless automation.

"To keep up, it took every ounce of strength and stamina our six-man crew could muster.

"In contrast to the cool million each of our guys were getting, the Colombians were paid $1,000 each, to off-load bales worth over $200,000 apiece. If any one of them were responsible for dropping a bale overboard, they knew they would pay with their life." From the expression on their faces, it was easy to see that pain was not unusual in their lives but rather a condition of it.

Each bale held forty individual one-kilo packages of coke which had been carefully sealed in thick plastic bags, then painfully wrapped in duct tape until they were thick and rigid. It was hoped this practice would keep any unwanted moisture out.

"No one on their boat spoke English but Shawn and I spoke a bit of Spanish, so we made out okay."

Each bale weighed 88 pounds, so transferring the load from the Colombian boat to their own in heavy seas was no small feat. "The wind grew with each passing hour so getting it all loaded as quickly as possible was imperative. By the time we finished the wind was pushing 25 knots and climbing."

As the sun had set a couple of hours earlier, Phil and his crew were left under pitch-black skies, with not as much as a partial moon to light their rails. "Our deck was cluttered with 2,586 kilos of cocaine worth between $200 and $300 million dollars, or put differently, it represented 101 bales, measuring three feet by five feet each.

"As it stood at the time, it was the largest shipment of cocaine ever brought into the Pacific Northwest," Phil stated proudly.

An average annual seizure in Canada would have been in the range of 100 to 150 kilos. This haul alone would exceed that which the Canadian authorities managed to intercept in any given year.

Without a break, the crew moved the load below deck, securing it as equally and tightly as possible in the port and starboard fuel compartments. In turn, Phil set a north-westerly course to pass between the Galapagos Islands and the Turks and Caicos Islands at 13 knots. His adrenaline was replaced with a nervous watch for unwanted traffic before it crossed their path.

"When it came to communication with Ralph or the club, we had been running in the dark since we left Victoria. While our on-board email system was there, I felt it best to keep all forms of communication to emergency use only," Phil explained.

There are two lines of thinking when it comes to smuggling. One was to hug the coast sixty miles offshore so you blend in with the general traffic moving north and south. Or, you move out to sea, perhaps six hundred miles well beyond the range of interdiction or halfway between the Hawaiian Islands and the U.S. mainland.

Phil chose the latter. "An overriding factor in this decision was the amount of fuel remaining on board. If I miscalculated there was no means to acquire fuel en route without inviting unwanted heat. It was therefore paramount that I not run out of diesel before we got home."

Once the interior fuel panels were sealed back into place, the chipped paint was touched up and all visual interference with the panels wiped clean, the heavy fishing gear was moved to block the panels. Easy access to the precious cargo would be all but impossible.

When it was Phil's turn to get some rest he set a 40-mile radius alarm on the ship's radar. Shawn was the most qualified to handle the helm during the night shift, on the understanding if the alarm was tripped, he would immediately wake Phil, who would then come to the wheelhouse and take charge until the situation had passed.

On the first night heading north, lights from another ship tested the ability of the alarm to react. Phil had no way of knowing whether it was the navy or the U.S. Coast Guard or just another fish boat like the *Western Wind*. It was half an hour before it came within range allowing Phil to relax and recognize it as a Japanese longliner. This happened more than once during their return trip and every time Phil's belly tightened until he confirmed all was well.

The *Western Wind's* headway was about 230 miles in a twenty-four hour period, so back in British Columbia, Ralph Harris knew he would hear nothing from Phil for at least two more weeks. As it was, Phil and the crew spent most of their return voyage fishing yellowfin tuna or mahi-mahi with rod and reel. If they were spotted from the air, they would appear legit. If they were stopped en route, they were hoping to have their hold full of fish, again setting prying eyes at ease.

On the fifth night, the ship's radar sounded with sodium lights from another ship breaking the horizon to the north. Phil assumed it was another fish boat, but he didn't know with certainty until there was a clear visual. It took thirty minutes before the gap had closed sufficiently to wipe away the thought of a Navy or Coast Guard ship.

That reckless conversation over channel 16 a few days earlier haunted his every hour. Phil will tell you, "The first ship you see on the return trip is always the worst," but for him none of them offered a sense of peace until they had faded beyond the aft horizon.

By the sixth day, they were smack in the middle of a school of bait fish balling up on the surface of the flat Pacific. The only sound was the hum of the engine keeping rhythm with the twist of the prop, until suddenly every reel screamed 'fish on'. They used large reels with a half mile of hundred-pound line. When tuna, mahi-mahi, or sailfish strike, they are travelling at seventy miles an hour, so the action is spontaneous.

Within seconds, every member of the crew was tethered to a safety line while clutching a rod and reeling for all they were worth. "It took fifteen minutes to get the first mahi on board," says Phil. "They were so big, they were un-nettable, so a second person had to abandon his rod to gaff or spear the first, then haul it on board." Before the hour had passed, the fish hold was starting to fill nicely.

There was never a lack of things to do while on board. Even though you were well out to sea, the engines required constant attention, whether it was a matter of greasing points of friction, changing fuel filters or a complete oil change.

Parallel to San Diego, but still 600 miles to the west, Phil noticed the weather fax projecting a not so pleasant storm coming on hard, two days in the near future.

"These systems start in the Pacific over Japan or China, so if you are watching your equipment, you have sufficient warning to alter your course or, depending on your experience, plow on through. In this case, the system was not of hurricane strength, but it was going to pack an eighty mile-per-hour punch, with a front that ran north of Los Angeles all the way to the upper reaches of Oregon. It was simply too big to escape with Cape Mendocino, California the centre of impact."

While Phil held the ship on course, the crew secured everything in and out of the ship, including the cooking pots, tin goods and cabinet doors in the kitchen, so nothing could turn into a missile when it struck.

By 6 p.m., a southeasterly hovered at 50 miles-per-hour while gusts reached 60. "On the Pacific, south-easterlies are always a killer, so by 2 a.m. the seas were thirty feet high with massive amounts of water dumping over our stern." While manageable for a ship of its size and with a captain of Phil's experience, it remained uncomfortable.

By noon the next day, the winds had increased to 80 miles-per-hour with gusts well in excess of that and it stayed that way over the next four days as the ship maintained a reduced speed of eight knots.

"As we sailed through the Pacific opposite the California coast, the waters were teaming with albacore tuna. Even in the heat of the storm our crew found great sport in fishing.

"The school they hooked into were not large as tuna go but were weighing in at eighteen to twenty-five pounds each. Even though the crew were clipped onto the jack line that ran fore and aft, when a giant wave thundered over the side, the guys had to watch each other's back.

"We had one case where the feet of the young kid we had on board were swept out from under him. As the water receded, I looked down from the bridge and here he was prone against the deck clinging for all he was worth to whatever metal his fingers could grip. One of his boots had been torn clear off his foot and flung-over the side. Had he not been tethered; we would have lost him for sure.

"When the wind exceeded 85 knots, all the hatches and doors were secured, with no one going outside. By then, the top layer of the ocean would lift off the main body of water four to six feet, such that I couldn't see the surface except intermittently. If anyone went overboard, there would be no way of recovering them."

With little to no sleep, Phil and his crew were just about spent. Try as they might, sleep was nearly impossible as the waves hammered the hull with the pitch and roll doing its best to slingshot the crew out of their bunks and onto the ceiling of their cabin.

By the time the storm abated, the *Western Wind* was roughly five days south of Canadian waters.

CHAPTER 14

Phil had developed several proven drop points along the west coast of Vancouver Island. Some were in First Nations waters where the RCMP were not welcome. With this load, he was looking further north to the area known as the Pacific Rim or more specifically, Ucluelet. But everything was subject to change right up until the last moment.

As the *Western Wind* made its way north, maritime law dictated it had to fall into the designated traffic lanes flowing north and south along the coast of Washington State. Phil also had to report to the Colombia River Marine Control Center, specifying his intended purpose and destination.

From that moment on, their ship was queued into the flow of traffic from the region. While physically, that area of the Pacific was within U.S. territorial waters, it was monitored by the Canadian Maritime Monitoring System. Sailing north, the Canadian Coast Guard would be the governing body he spoke with. That same authority would keep Phil updated on all the traffic around, in front and behind him. Much like an air-traffic controller, they would also advise him if another ship wanted to overtake his position. Their mandate was to keep everyone safe and unmolested.

As a ruse, Phil reported he would be turning east into the Straits of Juan de Fuca en route to Vancouver where he needed to off-load his fish, after which the ship would be pulled out of the water and repainted at the Shelter Island Marina. When work like this is done, the entire ship has to be enveloped in plastic sheets to contain paint flakes and protect the environment.

If he exercised this option, the *Western Wind* would be hidden inside the enclosure away from prying eyes, with the shipyard's gates closed and locked each night at 11:00 p.m. This granted Phil and his crew the freedom to cut a hole through each side of the ship, allowing for easy off-loading of the cocaine into a waiting truck. When the gates reopened at 6:00 a.m. he and his crew would drive out and make their way to the drop point forty minutes east.

"Each time I start one of these ventures," states Phil, "I have more than one option as to where I can drop my load. One of the easiest has been to engage a couple of smaller boats from Victoria, Sooke or Port Renfrew to meet me deep in open water during the dead of night.

"We'd off-load the cargo for them to transport to a destination other than my own. In reality there are a half dozen different ways to get the job done. But they all come saddled with a list of pros and cons. If all went well, Ralph and I would be filthy-rich in a couple of days.

"One of my problems is I have always lived large, so I never stayed filthy-rich for long."

In the meantime, the crew needed to fillet the fish they had on board, bag them and then pile them neatly into the commercial boxes so they could be off-loaded and sold prior to the ship being dry-docked.

Once on dry land it would be a number of days before the marina hooks the ship up to shore power. Any fish or food stuffs left on board would rot in no time and that would only invite the wrong noses to source out the root cause.

In no time the marine traffic had increased to a point where Phil was always within sight or sound of another vessel, whether it was a freighter or car carrier. The Tofino Coast Guard also saturated the airwaves giving instructions to the Canadian traffic.

"We had four VHF radios on board," says Phil, "each slotted into a different channel. One we used for our personal communication, another monitored the general traffic inclusive of the Pacific fishing fleet, a third was locked into the emergency channel 16 – which was mandatory for all ships our size – and the last one was glued to several of the military frequencies. I was able to hear U.S. and Canadian military vessels communicating with each other. In one case I listened to a U.S. nuclear submarine heading north out of the Bangor marine base, in Puget Sound."

Before they reached port, Phil wanted to remove two crew members from the ship so they would not be caught up in the venture if something went wrong. One was the kid who belonged to a friend of Phil's and who was far too young to be mixed up in this business and the second was the cook referred to as Red. Phil had prearranged with another fish boat to hook up with the *Western Wind* while off the Washington coastline and take them on board before he had to alter his course east into the Straits.

Two days south of his course change, Phil grabbed his Explorer email machine to send off a quick message to the bikers to confirm all was well with their point of rendezvous but the device crashed as soon as he hit the send button. Again and again this happened until he tossed it aside and accepted the future for what it was. He learned later that Red had spilled coffee on the machine the night before, but no one bothered to tell him.

Back in the comfort of his home Ralph Harris had no way of knowing what the final port of call would be or whether the crew had been arrested and confined.

Mid-afternoon and a hundred miles from his ship's course change, one of the large green military Aurora reconnaissance planes flying out of Comox passed low overhead. What had been looking like a promising trip suddenly took a turn for the worse. If the cops were coming, there was insufficient time to remove the tank panels, haul the dope to the upper deck and toss it over.

Phil went straight to the wheelhouse and checked the radar for enemy traffic. With a sigh of relief, he recognized all the targets on his screen as container ships. A few hours passed and nothing changed.

Still some distance from the Straits of Juan de Fuca, Phil called the Tofino Traffic control on his VHF radio, "Tofino Traffic this is Canadian vessel *Western Wind*". In a matter of seconds, the Coast Guard responded, "Good evening *Western Wind*, are you entering the traffic system tonight?" Phil replied, "Yes I am traffic."

Tofino Control asked for the boat's particulars, how many crew were on board and Phil's last port of call. As to the last port of call, he answered "Vancouver". As to his intended destination, he replied again, "Vancouver B.C., Canada". Following this the Coast Guard advised him as to who was behind him in the queue, then asked his estimated time of arrival to his next check point which would have been his course change east.

The outside world, including the RCMP and Coast Guard, now knew who he was, how many were with him and his intended destination. His pants were down around his ankles, so to speak, and his particulars exposed. At 2:30 the following morning, an outbound Canadian Navy frigate passed two miles off their port side. Phil watched them approach on his radar and automatically thought the worse. Had his crew been on deck at that time of the night they all would have leapt over the side and dog paddled for the Washington coast.

Moving at 10 knots with Cape Alava's flashing red light ahead and to the starboard side, Phil adjusted his course slightly to enter the northern half of the Straits of Juan de Fuca. There he would stay just long enough for his heading to register on the Tofino Control radar. The traffic outbound from the Straits began to bunch up in such a way that Phil hoped the control centre would lose him in the congestion. Assuming this was the case, he quickly corrected his course to his former heading with a fix on the Village of Ucluelet some 150 miles north by northwest.

Phil's heart sank when the Tofino Control addressed him once again, but relaxed when they asked if he had a visual on the larger ships which were meandering in and out of the traffic lanes like drunken sailors. Tofino had been trying to make contact with a couple of the freighter captains with no success. Phil responded, "Yes Tofino, I am monitoring them on radar along with the traffic on my aft starboard and am planning evasive action momentarily if they do not answer your calls in quick order."

As a couple of the ships maintained their collision course with the *Western Wind*, a Zodiac filled with gunmen darted past the corner of his right eye and turned sharp under his bow. His ill-feeling returned in a heartbeat and never left.

Before he had time to rationalize what was happening, Phil's radio crackled; "*Western Wind*, this is the U.S. Coast Guard. Stop your vessel," as three U.S. Coast Guard cutters came steaming down on him from the east.

With his mind groping for the best move, he withheld answering the dispatch. Reaching down to his right he opened the cabinet next to his wheelhouse chair, so he could pull out his .45 Smith & Wesson, along with a second pistol and his 12-gauge Winchester Defender shotgun.

He kept them within reach should South American pirates decide they liked the look of his ship enough to try and take it. As an extra precaution, Phil kept a number of diesel filled wine bottles mixed with soap and a rag stuffed down the throat of each. "The soap makes the fire from the explosion stick to everything it splatters on including human flesh."

He had no intention to shoot it out with the Americans, nor did he want the weapons on board when it came to a search. Being picked up in the U.S. with a gun in your possession is an automatic five-year term. A second gun will cost you an additional twenty-five years with no room for debate.

As he cut the fuel to the ship, Phil swung the rudder hard to the port leaving him a shield where he could throw the guns overboard without the Coast Guard being any the wiser.

"We were shocked when we learned that Stirling had continued with the operation after it was scuttled by our brass," says Pat Convey, "and here we learn that the *Western Wind* is heading back towards British Columbia and into the waiting arms of the Hells Angels with a huge cargo of cocaine. We were caught with our pants down so I notified the Americans as to what was about to happen with a request for them to intercept the ship as soon as it entered the Strait of Juan de Fuca."

But the U.S. agents wanted the bust to their credit, and they craved headlines, while Convey wanted to maintain the continuity of his earlier agreement and follow the load to its destination. In his opinion, "The ship, its crew and the load were small potatoes in comparison to nabbing not only the load, but the kingpins who financed the operation along with their larger bankroll."

During the evening of February 21, 2001, a swat team of twenty men in full combat gear, mixed with a handful of DEA agents in their nicely pressed white shirts and monogrammed hats, scaled the sides of the ship with AR-15s pointed at anyone who dared to breathe.

Some of the crew were sleeping below deck so they missed out on all the theatrics. Before someone started blabbing in a sleepy stupor, Shawn slipped below to make certain no one spoke when confronted. By law they were not obliged to offer anything other than their names and place of residence.

"Anything more would make things difficult for the rest of us," Phil said, speaking from experience.

"The young lad never had a chance to flee the eventuality, but in all honesty, he proved himself more of a man than most of our remaining crew. His father would have been proud of the way he conducted himself."

The DEA's opening line as they burst into the wheelhouse was, "How many people on board?" To which Phil calmly replied, "five".

One by one, the crew members were cuffed and led out onto the deck where they were made to sit on the salt encrusted hatch that covered the fish holds with temperatures hovering in the high 40s. By then, there was a second boatload of well-armed men clamouring over the side of their ship.

There was not a single member of the Canadian forces in sight, leaving Phil to ponder what the hell the Americans were doing when taking such action was against international law, without permission from their Canadian counterpart. "We knew the Americans often ignore international law, as well as their own laws, if it seems expedient to their cause."

As if by design, the bilge alarm rang in the wheelhouse and engine room. It was a normal occurrence that happened every three or four days, but this time it brought about a state of panic with the cops hollering, "What's wrong? What's wrong?"

Eventually some guy came up to Phil, stuck a gun in his face and demanded he shut the thing off. Quick as a whip, Phil responded, "Then you'd better let the engineer out of his cuffs and into the engine room before something really bad happens. I'm not the engineer, I'm the captain and the engineer handles that stuff, not me."

To add to the mayhem, Tofino Control came on the radio demanding to know what was going on. "They could see a cluster of five boats on their radar tucked in tight beside us and that we were drifting towards the Cape Alava reef, which by that time was only 100 yards off our starboard rail."

Phil looked over at the customs officer. "What do you want me to do?"

Was he going to bother answering Tofino or restart the ship and move away from the reef or both? Based on the proximity of the flashing marker the cop had no more than three minutes to decide.

Not only would the reef punch a hole in the side of the *Western Wind*, it would dump diesel and engine oil all over the region. On the plus side, the evidence would go down with the ship thereby closing the case before it truly opened.

Phil was instructed to answer Tofino.

"Tofino Coast Guard this is the *Western Wind*. I have been boarded by an American Swat team, the U.S. DEA and the FBI, plus God only knows who else. They have no warrant and I have not authorized these people to come on board. I do not care who they are or what they want, but I have 50 guns pointed at me right now so I am unable to tell you what is about to happen, as they will not allow me to operate my ship. I have a Canadian registered vessel with a Canadian crew, standing here under duress while flying a Canadian flag. I am asking for assistance."

Irate, one of the DEA grabbed the microphone out of Phil's hand to suppress any further discourse, but the damage was done. All Coast Guard communications, whether they be Canadian, or U.S. are recorded and held on file indefinitely.

"*Western Wind*, we heard you, but your position and the position of the other vessels around you are dangerously close to the reef and we strongly advise you to take evasive action." By then the flashing marker was about 100 feet away.

Phil turned to the guy hovering over him, "Hey buddy, we're going to be abandoning ship in less than a minute if you don't do something about our position." Sweat was pouring off the guy's forehead. Phil could tell he was no mariner and had no clue as to what was about to happen.

The question was bouncing around in the back of Phil's mind; *Who was it that ratted us out?*

Finally, the guy hovering over Phil snapped to and told him, "Move the boat."

With the rocks only a few feet off the starboard rail, Phil responded with his best poker face, "You have pirated my ship without proper authorization from anyone in Canada, while I am within international traffic lanes. I'm not doing anything until the cuffs are removed from my crew and they are allowed back inside to the galley table."

The guy turned and yelled out the door to those guarding the crew to remove their cuffs and escort them in.

Showing no concern for the smaller craft bunched up around the *Western Wind*, Phil hit the throttle while cranking the rudder hard to port, barely avoiding the rocks as he made his way out into deeper water.

With the ship back in deep water, the guy that followed Shawn down to the engine room and the one that stood over Phil, took their leave onto the outer deck so they could have a private conversation. This gave Shawn and Phil an opportunity to put Plan B into play.

In the event their ship was overtaken, Shawn and Phil had mapped out a sequence of events that would follow. Assuming they were over the 600-foot trench that ran parallel with the coast, and they were both free of observation, Phil would trip the fire alarm while Shawn returned to the engine room and broke open the twelve-inch diameter sea water intake, which was adjacent to the fresh water holding tank.

It fed sea water to the fish hold and all it would take was one good blow with the sledgehammer on the pipe's elbow as it ran through the ship's hull. "We kept the sledgehammer leaning against the wall nearby for just that reason. Once done, nobody would be able to damper the flood. Within fifteen minutes the *Western Wind* with all its evidence would be sitting on the bottom of the Pacific."

Problem was, Phil still needed ten minutes or so before he would be over the trench but the cops returned to their respective positions.

The head guy turned to Phil and asked, "Where are the drugs, Phil?" To which Phil replied, "What drugs?" The conversation at this point became tit for tat with the DEA. "Don't play stupid with us, we know you have drugs on board." Phil responded, "I don't have shit, no guns, no drugs, no nothing. We are heading to Canada with our load of fish, so what the hell are you doing here?"

The cop came right back at him, "We're going to cut the ship into little pieces if you don't tell us where it is." As per the script, Phil replied, "I have no idea what you are talking about." That was the last piece of dialogue between them for fourteen hours as the reserve battalion crawled over the ship from stem to stern.

It wasn't long before one of the cops came forward with handwritten notes he'd found in Phil's cabin. He gave them to Donald Bambenek, the senior U.S. Customs special agent. The notes explained how to transmit and receive coded emails with the Hells Angels, plus the co-ordinates for the rendezvous point with the Colombians, along with the precise meeting time and date. Phil's ability to deny there were drugs on board was rapidly diminishing.

The Americans had spent hours drilling holes in every bulkhead and interior panel they could find, so they could peer in and see what was hidden behind, but they still had not uncovered any drugs. Every twenty minutes through the night they would ask Shawn to pump out the fish hold or shut down the water and fuel supply but he refused to do anything without first receiving permission from Phil, his captain.

The Coast Guard had their own engineer on board, but he was nervous about touching anything for fear of sinking the ship or worse, so this gave Phil and Shawn frequent opportunities to converse.

An older DEA veteran came on board. Phil figured he was well beyond retirement age. He was tall and thin with stark white hair, the likes of what you get when you have been in the heat of things far too long. Phil was watching him closely and figured his charade had finally come to an end when this guy pulled a tape measure out of his windbreaker pocket and began to measure the breadth of the ship's upper deck.

This old guy figured out there was space below deck that had not been accounted for by his peers. From there the veteran agent opened the forward hatch and peered down at all the fishing gear piled against the side panels.

He called over a couple of the higher-ranking agents. Their discussion lasted only a few minutes with the others clearly not supporting the older man's theory. The conversation ended when the guy who had threatened Phil walked into the wheelhouse and announced the *Western Wind* was going to be towed into Port Angeles where they would use a torch to cut it to pieces.

Cocky as ever, Phil told them to go ahead. "I have no drugs on board and no idea what you are talking about." They then asked Shawn for some tools, to which he replied, "Go find them yourself."

By then it was raining and the whole lot were cold and drenched. Phil held onto a slim ray of hope that the cops would just leave out of frustration and allow him to get underway, but this would not prove to be the case.

One of the DEA agents took Shawn below to the engine room. He and Phil still held to the notion they might find an opportunity to break open the water line, but their ship was still shy of the 600-foot trench. Anything less and the ship would be sitting in shallow enough water to allow easy extraction of the drugs. The two never had to speak. They knew what was required and fully understood how Phil would signal when they were on target. After that, it was up to Shawn if he had the freedom to swing the hammer.

At this point Phil could see another ship fast approaching from Canadian waters. It turned out to be the Canadian Navy out of Esquimalt Harbour with a couple of RCMP officers on board.

With the Americans running amok over the ship, the RCMP stood watch from the bridge of the Canadian frigate and did nothing. Phil could see one of them with a cell phone to his ear but was unable to see if it was Convey with his pal or some other cop hoping to introduce himself to a piece of the action. He had no way of knowing if they were working on his behalf or jockeying for a fragment of the glory if it fell from the U.S. grip. Either way, the authorities were confident they were about to witness a seizure of the largest shipment of cocaine in the history of the Pacific Northwest.

Finally, a lone DEA officer took his senior counterpart seriously, jumped into the forward hold and started tossing the fishing gear up onto the deck. The netting was far too heavy for one man, so two others joined in. Their flurry of activity continued for an hour.

Phil knew they were going to need a wrench to remove the 140 nuts from off the two fuel tank enclosures, but he was loath to offer them a speck of help. They were just going to have to come up with the tool on their own.

As he looked down from the wheelhouse he knew it was only a matter of time until all their dirty secrets would be exposed to the outside world.

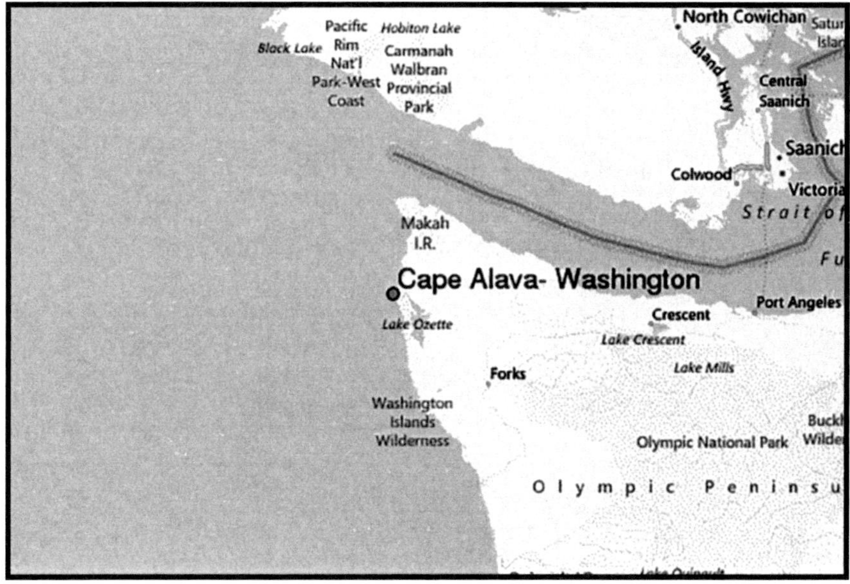

Map of Cape Alava, Washington State.

Cape Alava - Washington State.

Phil Stirling in wheelhouse of *Western Wind*.

Western Wind.

CHAPTER 15

As expected, before long the first brick of cocaine came up on deck. The old agent pulled out his pocketknife and cut into it. As he did, the fates of Ralph, Phil and his crew took a dramatic turn for the worse.

Not only had the duo lost their life's savings, they had lost any posture they might have held within the underworld, in their families, their neighbours and friends, but most definitely within the public at large, a segment that the media would play up to.

Special Agent Rodney Tureaud of the U.S. Customs, Seattle office, was over the top as he knew he had nabbed the largest cocaine bust the region had ever seen. His head was spinning as to how to make the most out of the six o'clock news, for each media outlet would be bidding for the best sound bites. Tureaud had previously shot his mouth off that he had three goals in life. He wanted to seize a helicopter or plane which was in the act of smuggling. Then he wanted to nail a dogsled of all things, again involved in smuggling. And lastly, he wanted to take down a member of the Hells Angels so he could wave their colours in front of the cameras as some kind of trophy.

Word had it he was yet to nab the dogsled. Had he been tuned into the activities of Ralph's old friend Lou Brown, whose teenage son had been transporting B.C. bud across the border south of Nelson since he was a teenager, first strapping the drugs to his back on weekends and during school's summer break, before turning to snowmobiles and sleds during the winter months, he might have managed to check off one of his objectives.

Tureaud could have been party to the DEA sting that scooped Sam Brown in February of 2009 when at the age of 24 he had piloted a stolen helicopter into a remote site in northern Washington with more pot than the cops could ever imagine, 83 kg of cocaine, 240,000 ecstasy tablets, plus cash, and guns, all slung beneath the bird.

Having the last word, Tureaud added, “When moments like this fall in your lap, you don’t have time to call Washington and ask ‘Mother, may I?’ You act and you act fast, or the opportunity passes you by.”

The DEA’s next order of business was to remove Phil from the wheelhouse and station him under guard in the galley with the remainder of his crew. With an innate calmness, Phil gestured to the crew that all would be well as long as they remained silent. He would not hang them out to dry and this was not so much their problem as it was his.

Twenty minutes later, he was cuffed and brought back into the wheelhouse. The U.S. Customs official who had taken charge, by that time pressed him for where the coke was heading and who the ultimate buyer might be. Silence is all Phil offered in return.

As this unfolded, a skiff from off the Canadian ship pulled up alongside the *Western Wind* and added the two men in dark trench coats and fedoras to the already overcrowded ship. The guy who was badgering Phil in the wheelhouse left him alone and joined the two Canadians on the main deck.

One fellow was clearly a grunt, while the other was a representative of Canada’s Witness Protection Program. The rain had stopped so their discussion was not as uncomfortable as it would have been earlier.

No additional kilos were brought up from the forward hold. It seemed the one they had was sufficient to satisfy their immediate needs, but their excitement had caused them once again to forget about the ever-present Cape Alava reef now a quarter mile off their stern.

Phil was watching it on the ship’s radar, creeping closer and closer with each passing moment. Under the circumstances, having the rocks tear open the side of the ship wouldn’t be the worst thing that could happen since Phil and Ralph could always redeem some of their loss against the ship’s marine policy.

Eventually the U.S. Customs came back into the wheelhouse with their cell phones still pressed to their ears. When their private conversations ended, one informed Phil, “We know the Hells Angels are waiting for you at the Cheanuh Marina on the Canadian side and we want you to deliver the load to them as planned. But first we want you to email them and tell them you are going to be a couple of days late. This will allow your RCMP friends to get into position and make the arrests.”

That was news to Phil as he had only set his mind on Ucluelet as the point to off-load moments before the Coast Guard arrived. As for his final destination, he had not been able to connect with Ralph or the bikers via email because his computer was defunct.

Ralph Harris recalled the frenzied activity that ensued.

"I received a call early that morning from Sheppe saying that he and Juel Stanton, with two others were heading to Cheanuh Marina to meet Phil. Somehow, he had received word that Phil had chosen it as a drop point, but he refused to say how he came by that information.

"I jumped into my truck and headed straight for the marina. When I arrived, I could see Lea Sheppe and his friends loitering about the docks wearing their club colours for all to see. They were so engrossed in watching for the *Western Wind* to round the point of land that they were oblivious to the dozen or so cops who were doing their best to stay hidden among the RV trailers at the top of the hill.

"I drove straight to the boat ramp and told Sheppe about the cops but he insisted they were not a worry, since 'I told you they had been paid off'. He told me I had no place being there and to get lost or there would be hell to pay, so I left."

This confirmed that no one on board was the rat and it was unlikely Ralph, as he had no way of knowing what Phil's final intentions were. Lea Sheppe, however, knew all that had been planned and it was he who insisted on two occasions that the venture proceed even though Ralph had advised him against it.

"I know for a fact," stated Ralph, "that my everyday phone was tapped on February 5, 2001 and remained that way until December 31, 2003. I was real cautious as to what I said over any of my phones and always insisted on a face to face when meeting with the bikers.

"Like most of my peers, I had a series of burn phones. Ones that you purchase at the corner store with a set number of minutes on them and the determination that they will be destroyed the moment they are used for something incriminating. But this didn't stop the likes of Sheppe from saying whatever over my regular phone without first putting his brain into gear."

While viewed by Phil and Ralph as a smokescreen, the official release stated that: "A member of the Canadian's Coastal Watch program had reported suspicious activity on the vessel two months earlier. The Canadian authorities alerted the U.S. Coast Guard only as a courtesy and the boat seizure was by pure chance."

Whether the Coastal Watch tuned into the Colombian Captain's outburst on the international channel 16 or not, no one will say, but the official timing leaves it suspect.

Nonetheless, Phil Stirling viewed this as a confirmation the RCMP wanted to salvage their original plan and their agreement with him was still on the table. At that moment, it seemed like the best option.

Phil demanded that his cuffs and those on Shawn's wrists be removed so they could prepare the ship to get underway. The Customs officer barked, "No way is your engineer being released. You either do it on your own or you're going to jail, I don't care either way."

Not one to shy away from a good debate, Phil reacted sharply: "None of you goons can run this ship and I can't run it without him, so if he isn't with me, your great plan isn't going to happen. Furthermore, if the bikers at the marina don't see my face on deck as we arrive, they will scatter like feral cats into the forest behind the marina."

At that point the cop left the wheelhouse and reunited with the two Canadians on the main deck. As they talked, they kept their gaze on Phil in the wheelhouse as though he was about to up and vanish. Eventually one of the agents moved towards the back of the ship and brought Shawn forward without his cuffs.

When the Customs guys left them alone, Phil shared their demands about delivering the dope to the bikers. With limited time together, he reassured Shawn this was not going to happen, but rather Plan B would play out when the ship was over the trench six miles northeast of their current position.

They both understood that once the pipe was separated from the hull it would only take ten minutes for the ship to start sinking and at that point it would be every man for himself. They all knew the survival suits were within easy reach and there were plenty of them to go around.

Shawn told Phil the entire crew were good, except for Red the cook. "He is an idiot and will sell us all out the first chance he gets."

By the time the ship got underway, the reef's flashing light was a scant 100 feet off the starboard rail. Even though Phil was behaving as instructed, the cops stood there with stunned looks on their faces, uncertain as to what their next move would be. You could slice the tension in the air with a butter knife.

The Customs guy who appeared to be the one in charge, motioned for Phil to come out onto the upper deck. When Phil cooperated, the guy wanted to know how long it was going to take to get to the Cheanuh Bay Marina. Phil knew it would take about eight hours at top speed but suggested in less than polite terms, they should consult their own captains on such matters, not the man who they are holding hostage.

Shawn came back into the wheelhouse just as the U.S. and Canadian guys started yelling at each other. Dialogue between the two groups had meandered well beyond cordial. The DEA disliked what the Canadian boys had to say. Phil could pick up broken sentences as the Americans held nothing back when telling their Canadian counterparts they were a pack of half-wits. Through the entire tirade, the Canadians kept their cell phones to their ears. There was a strong sense in the air that this had turned into an international foray and plans were about to change.

One of the Canadians had been on the line with Pat Convey, who in turn had Inspector Richard Barszczewski, the officer in charge of the B.C. Drug Enforcement Division, on another line. Convey was once again trying to convince his superior that the cost of entrapping the bikers was well worth a million dollars, but Barszczewski had already turned the proposal down and was having no part of it now, no matter how stupid it made the RCMP look.

The U.S. cops suggested that they had the manpower and the logistics to make the delivery as planned, but they needed Barszczewski's authority to operate on Canadian soil. Even though it would not cost the Canadians a dime, Barszczewski balked once again.

Without Barszczewski, any form of witness protection or for that matter, a money deal, was off the table. His inaction has gone on record as one of the biggest blunders in Canada's war against organized crime. Once again, the RCMP brass had blown the case but that wouldn't get in the way of Barszczewski receiving a substantial promotion.

Convey was outraged. "It was a good international bust and the wheels not only fell off, but they kept falling off. All those involved, including Stirling, were stunned at Barszczewski's actions." Barszczewski has declined to offer any justification, except to say, "It's not right for me to talk about it." This was a prime example of a government agency at contretemps.

Tureaud, the American agent, was livid.

"It was a travesty. For two or three small rocks of crack cocaine – something you can put on a single fingertip – you go to jail in the U.S. for ten or more years. We catch a boatload of two and a half tonnes of cocaine and the Canadians turn them loose. It's baffling.

"We had an opportunity to make a significant impact on organized crime in the U.S. and Canada. It's an insult to everybody in law enforcement on both sides of the border. It is not a rationalization that sits well with the Americans. We on the ground level who are working the case should be allowed to go forward with it. You don't stop doing the case to cover your ass."

Phil and Shawn had a problem all their own. They were now forty minutes from the point where Plan B had to be exercised or forgotten. The entire time this was playing out, one of the U.S. cops stood in the doorway to the galley where the remaining crew were retained, his machine gun at post and an expression on his face that suggested he was void of emotion. The sad and scary part about this image is that the guy had no idea how stupid he looked. Instead, he just stood there acting proud and arrogant. In his mind he was a display of a tough guy fighting bad guys. His finger was resting beside the trigger, so one wrong word and he might have a mind to start shooting.

While standing on the main deck, the Customs agent in charge ordered Phil to bring his ship to a full stop as the Canadian frigate inched its way closer to the *Western Wind*. A decision had been made and Phil was about to find out what it was.

Still holding to Plan B, he chose to not hear the order and continued driving his ship forward. A minute or so later, the radio strapped to his guard's chest crackled to life "If you do not stop this ship now, this guard has orders to shoot you."

That seemed straight forward enough so he pulled the throttle back into its off position and then waited for the ship to come to a halt before sliding the gears into neutral. Ships of this size don't stop on a dime so Phil was hoping the guy with the itchy trigger finger would have enough intelligence to realize this.

Once stopped, the Canadian vessel sent their Zodiac to pick up their two colleagues. Like a couple of old maids who had been spanked by their American counterparts, they made their way down the ship's ladder, almost falling headfirst into the arms of the navy boys below. They were not comfortable being in such a small craft on choppy seas, nor were they happy at having their tailored suits drenched by the saltwater spraying over the sides.

With the Canadians heading back to the safety of their desks, a U.S. Coast Guard Zodiac pulled up alongside the *Western Wind*. Out hopped a guy dressed all in white. If he had a few more pounds on him, he could have played the part of Mr. Clean in the commercials. He immediately huddled with the cops on the main deck, again with their focus in Phil's direction.

Shawn was removed from the wheelhouse by the cop with the machine-gun, as the officer in white, the head Customs guy and the lead DEA agent, made their way to Phil. The DEA agent made it known that he was taking over control of the *Western Wind* and that Phil was to join his crew in the galley. Unlike the other cops, the guy in white turned out to be a mariner.

"Twenty minutes later, I was summoned back to the wheelhouse where I was informed the Coast Guard captain was unable to engage the drive gear, nor did he understand the navigation program that I had running on the ship's computer and lastly, he was dumbfounded as to how to disengage it from the autopilot.

"The navigational program was your basic NAVTEC program with thousands of copies sold throughout the world and this guy didn't know how to operate it? You had to wonder what kind of training they are giving the U.S. captains these days."

Phil spoke with his less than cooperative reply, "And what do you want from me?"

The DEA agent suggested, "Captain, it would be in your best interests and that of your crew if you were to drive the ship."

"Why? What's in it for me?"

DEA: "Well, we might give the ship back to you."

Fat chance! When pigs fly, Phil thought.

Phil asked: "Are you attempting to make the delivery?"

DEA: "The Canadians have botched the deal so there will be no delivery."

Phil: "Okay, get out of the way. Where are we going?"

Coast Guard: "Port Angeles."

"Then tell your Coast Guard vessel on our starboard side to move out of my way and use channel 72 VHF for contact."

Without seeking permission, Phil radioed Tofino Marine Control to advise them of the situation. "*Western Wind*, we have now been arrested by the Americans. Please make special note that we are a Canadian registered vessel and have been boarded without permission from me, under duress and at gunpoint while against our will, we are being forced to make our way to Port Angeles in the United States."

No one on board attempted to intervene.

It was midday as they pulled up to the Coast Guard dock in Port Angeles to a crowd of curiosity seekers. Media photographers were snapping pictures of the ship's exterior as though it would have some monetary value downstream.

As Phil and his crew were cuffed and led down the gangway to a common holding cell within the Coast Guard headquarters, the clicking of camera shutters erupted into a frenzy.

David Giles, aka Gyrator on the right.

Cargo on the *Western Wind*.

CHAPTER 16

I had no idea Phil had been intercepted until it hit the news that evening," Ralph Harris would explain much later. "I had no communication with him whatsoever since he left Victoria to head south.

"Within an hour of the broadcast, I had received a call from Sheppe with no veiled threat that someone was going to have to pay for the load and it wasn't going to be the Colombians. I reminded him that he had been advised twice that the cops were onto him and that he insisted on plowing ahead just the same. But he was the last man on earth to assume responsibility when things went wrong."

As Phil and his crew were led away, five Coast Guard agents presented comic relief as they shimmied up the aft flagpole of the *Western Wind* in an attempt to remove the ship's gravel truck sized Canadian flag. Once up, they were stymied by the complex array of knots securing the flag in place. It appeared the U.S. agents had serious concern over how the media's portrayal of a Canadian ship under siege may come back to bite them.

Shawn didn't help matters as he threw a steady stream of expletives at them over their total disregard for the Canadian flag. In contrast, if he was to tamper with an American flag, no matter what the circumstances, the U.S. would come unglued and justify it as grounds for an armed conflict.

Phil knows Shawn better than Shawn knows himself. Whereas Phil will keep almost everything to himself, if it's on Shawn's mind, it's going to come out and not always with discretion and regard for who may be listening.

However, that act with their flag contributed more towards Phil and his crew gaining their freedom, than anything else.

Once confined, Phil had a chance to tutor his crew on what to expect. But before he started he made it known that the room likely contained listening devices so conversation should be limited to the last good movie they enjoyed or meal they ate.

Phil assured them they would all receive good lawyers, "so stay calm and stay quiet." For those who had never been exposed to the American way, he made certain each knew they were entitled to a phone call and that their interrogators were not their friends, regardless of suggestions otherwise. "Anything said will be twisted and used against you, along with your fellow crewmates," Shawn counselled. "Foul up and you will spend the next hundred years as a sex toy in some remote U.S. prison."

The entire lot knew they would be subjected to questioning, not unlike that of international terrorists. The investigators had shrinks on retainer who would guide them in what and how to ask the most pressing questions and what force could be applied under current law. While Phil dreaded the thought, he didn't fear it. As for the balance of the crew – Shawn excluded –they knew very little about what had preceded and transpired during their voyage or who the load was acquired for. So, there was little fear of them being broken.

Not surprising, the kid was the first to be led off for interrogation, but he was gone less than three minutes. Frank was next.

Red, the cook, demanded of the kid, "Where did they take you?" The kid replied, "They asked me to rat everyone out and I told them to stick it where the sun don't shine, I'm not saying nothin' to nobody."

While Phil was ashamed for getting the kid into this situation, he had watched him grow into a man right before his eyes. As for the rest of the crew, they were all adults and knew full well the risk they were taking when they signed on. So, those were the breaks.

Frank returned after a few minutes as well, giving them nothing other than a request to speak with his lawyer.

Red followed. Unlike the situations with Frank and the kid, Red was gone for well over an hour. Finally, the kid said what everyone else was thinking, "I think Red is ratting us all out." Phil assured him, "Red knows little to nothing worth sharing." Shawn added, "One person testifying against us can't do anything. They will need far more than that. Besides, the prosecutor will soon recognize Red as the dumb stick he is and the fact that he will not make a good witness."

Shawn was next but everyone knew that while he may be a drunk most of the time, he was a veteran when it came to interdiction. Five minutes later, the interrogators were back with Shawn and it was Phil's turn.

Phil was led down the hall and when the door to the interrogation room opened there was the old DEA narc with two others he had not seen before. All were dressed in dark suits and sitting behind an old desk, Gestapo style, in a semi-dark room. All that was missing was the high intensity lamp swinging back and forth over the victim's chair.

Out of the shadows walked Pat Convey, in the same trench coat he always wore. It didn't matter the time of day, the place or the event, Pat always wore the same clothes. "Hi Phil. Well you're in big shit now. I'm not going to play around with you, so you can either testify against the Hells Angels and everyone in Colombia, the U.S. and Canada that you know, or you will serve the next seven years down here in a U.S. prison."

"Take me to jail," was Phil's only response.

You had to hand it to Convey, no matter how many times his superiors threw him under the bus, he would dust himself off and try one more time to get Phil's cooperation.

Phil's reply ended the interrogations, so he was led back to the holding cell where everyone remained except for 'Red the Rat' – a new name given to him by his crewmates.

Before a whole lot of time had passed, Phil and his crew were escorted out of the building into a waiting van and driven to the SeaTac Federal Detention Centre just outside of Seattle, where they would await a bail hearing, a trial or whatever else the U.S. court system threw at them.

They were ushered into a large room where representatives of the Bureau of Prisons, the DEA, and U.S. Customs were actively and loudly engaged in a heated argument. Each was trying to express their authority by telling the other how things were going to play out. It was complete mayhem.

Phil interrupted the ruckus and requested an opportunity to make a call, but the Customs agent denied him flatly and then insisted they all be detained separately. At this point, the representative from the Bureau of Prisons reminded the others whose building they were standing in, thereby making him the ultimate authority and for that reason alone, he would take no direction from any of them. He turned to the Customs agent, "You want to stop the phone call? Then you'll need a court order. Do ya have one of those?" One at a time he dialed the crew's requested number and allotted each man fifteen minutes to relay their message into the receiver. In an attempt to calm their spirits, most took the opportunity to speak with a family member.

Phil had dreaded putting the receiver to his ear. He could tell by Marlene's hesitation that she had already seen the news. Then she exploded. "My God Phil, you are all over the TV. The newspapers are camped out in our driveway. There must be 100 of them with their cars and trucks all the way down to the road. I can hardly get out of our home and every time I do, cameras are flashing.

"Even my mother and sister in Toronto know about it because it's on all the news channels, twenty-four hours a day. That is all I hear and see. The neighbours are looking at me like you're either the head of the Mafia or Charles Manson. Not sure which. Where are you? Are you okay?"

He answered her questions calmly, then she added, "One of your good friends stopped by and said you are all getting a good lawyer who will be there in the morning."

As the calls wrapped up, a tall blonde woman approached Phil identifying herself as a representative of the Canadian Consulate, sent to ensure they were being treated well. Accompanying her were two Canadian cops who appeared to be acting as bodyguards. This was a shock to Phil as he had never heard of the Canadian government lifting a finger for Canadians detained outside their borders.

Phil enquired what it was she was going to do for them but she had no definitive answer. When asked if she or one of the Canadian agencies had authorized the U.S. forces to storm a Canadian ship, she stated she had no knowledge of it. When he asked what she or her representatives were going to do about the U.S. boarding a Canadian vessel while flying a Canadian flag, and clearly identifying their destination as being in Canada, she said there was nothing she could do.

Again, Phil asked, "Then what are you here for?"

The woman replied, "To help in any way I can."

Phil had the last word. "Then why, when I ask for your assistance in the two most crucial areas of our confinement, you are either unable or, more likely, unwilling to assist?"

All she could do was shrug her shoulders.

By this time, the crew members were heated and addressing her in terms not considered politically correct. Without hesitation, the two bodyguards moved forward, cradled each arm and hustled her out of the room while slamming the door behind them. The U.S. guys enjoyed every minute of the interaction and began laughing in the faces of Phil and his crew.

The bureau supervisor informed them they were going to be cuffed and shackled, then separated. While the crew was led in one direction, Phil was led in another. He was directed to a room where a rather large black man dressed in a Bureau uniform was waiting. There he was unshackled and told to change into a prison jump suit. "It was tattered, dirty, faded and well beyond its years of normal use, plus it smelled like rotten eggs," Phil recalls.

"Let's go Cracker Boy," the big guy said, after replacing his cuffs and shackles. Down the hallway and up in an elevator they went. When it stopped, he was ushered into one of the smallest cells he had ever seen. "You could hardly turn around in it. I've been in solitary confinement that was more spacious, plus the lights were kept on 24/7 and it came with no blanket or pillow.

"Each night, the air was filled with the sound of some nutcase a couple of doors down going off on his imaginary friend. In reality, I was likely doing penance, as the guy was clearly going through withdrawal. The thought did cross my mind that it might have been a recording they used to break their prisoners."

Come morning, an even larger, ugly guy, white this time, with a southern accent, took Phil to the elevator, then down to the main floor where he was ordered to change back into his street clothes. He was offered coffee and a bun, after which he was abandoned in a standard cell for an hour or so.

Eventually the Custom's officer from the ship, with the older DEA agent, entered the room and offered Phil a bullet proof vest. He told them where they could stuff it, as he would not be wearing it. They gave him the option to put it on, or they would put it on for him. Phil gave in to their request. After the cuffs and chains were replaced, they left the building.

Waiting outside were a group of guards in swat gear, pointing shotguns in the direction of thirty to forty newspaper and TV crews restrained behind ropes on the opposite side of the road. It took Phil a minute or two to realize the vest and guards were part of an elaborate charade to make him appear as though he was a protected informant. They were sending the bikers a message that could only add pressure to Phil's already untenable situation.

From there, Phil was driven to the secure underground parking of the Seattle courthouse where he was placed in a holding cell. Two other cells were occupied, but not with members of his crew.

One by one the other prisoners were led away but they never returned. Three hours passed before Phil was finally offered coffee in a paper cup that within minutes became saturated and leaked badly.

Two hours later, the main door to the cells opened allowing a guard to walk in. This gave Phil a chance to ask if there was going to be court that morning. All the guard would say was, "The lawyers are arguing about something and the judge ain't real happy about it, while all the press and TV people are soaking it up."

Phil had not seen a lawyer, so none of this made sense.

It was seven and a half hours from the time Phil arrived at the courthouse before a guard returned. "You must be one of the luckiest guys in the world," then turned with a smile and walked out.

Next through the door came the all too familiar Customs officer and the older DEA agent who had found the hidden cache of drugs. Their faces betrayed them as having just had their asses handed to them on a platter. Their eyes were bloodshot, their faces supported a three-day stubble, and they were wearing the same salt-encrusted clothes they had on aboard the *Western Wind* two days earlier. They had definitely been beaten up by the judge or prosecutor or both.

They opened Phil's cell, put the cuffs on his wrists, but not the shackles and then led him to the check-out counter where a man from U.S. Immigration and Customs Enforcement wrote him a $150 ticket for illegally entering the country.

It was a quiet ten-minute ride to the immigration jail where he was about to become a resident. "When I arrived, the two guys never even bothered to get out and open the car door for me, they just pulled in behind the security gates and let one of the resident officers take over."

The immigration officer apparently knew what had just happened and with a chuckle asked, "Had a rough day Captain? Your crew are inside waiting for you. I will get you something to eat if you like?"

"Frank was missing from our group. Because he was First Nations, they had no choice but to let him walk out of the courthouse with a one-way ticket home," Phil theorized.

A short time later the ICE officer returned to take them for processing. After they had changed into prison attire, they were led to the kitchen galley where they were fed beans with rice, and then they were escorted to their rooms.

"Shawn and I were stuck in a room with a hundred Mexicans and one guy from Norway. The Norwegian had just completed his term for smuggling drugs and was being shipped back to his homeland." The room was dirty and stunk.

On day two, British Columbia lawyer Jennifer McCormick arrived in the company of a second lawyer appointed by the Seattle judge. Phil had met Jennifer in 1989. She had been the prosecutor that put him away for five years. Since then, she had opened her own practice and became what Phil referred to as, "a good friend. I held no grudges," says Phil. "She was just doing her job."

Since he hadn't summoned her, he asked, "What the hell are you doing here?" Increasing the wattage of her smile while cocking her head to one side, she responded with equal strength, "I just thought I would come down to help you. You're in a lot of trouble and I thought maybe I could help somehow."

Phil couldn't put aside the feeling that she was there with ulterior motives. To his mind 'true' and 'pretty true' are not the same thing and he was confident her words fell into the latter category.

Lady Justice has her eyes blindfolded, not so she can provide an unbiased rendering, but because she can't bear to watch the corrupt games her underlings play each day as they attempt to manipulate their targets.

The American courts were unable to tie him, the *Western Wind*, the cocaine and the crew together with a common thread and unless they could there would be no case. Was Jennifer a puppet for the DEA or Customs? Was she sent by the RCMP to twist his words into a testimony that could be used against him when he returned home? One thing he knew for sure was that he had established no lawyer/client relationship with Jennifer so any of the many possibilities were on the table. From that moment forward, he knew with certainty, if her lips moved, it had to be a lie.

While Shawn was standing before the Seattle judge, the DEA, FBI and U.S. Customs had jointly tried to convince the judge that the *Western Wind* had not been registered to a country thereby making it a 'stateless vessel' and subject to charges under the 'Piracy and Felony Clause of the U.S. Constitution'.

Using this as leverage, Jennifer and the U.S. appointed lawyer had concocted a plea deal where Phil would only serve seven years. "They made it sound like they were doing me a favour. But along with the seven years, I would still have to testify against everyone involved, including my crew."

Only later would he learn that Jennifer had been given a free ride south on the RCMP chopper courtesy of Pat Convey. She had been tasked with the mission of convincing Phil to cooperate in exchange for a lighter sentence. "The entire time this performance was being played out, Convey had been watching through the mirrored glass on one wall of the interrogation room."

Pat Convey adds a different view of what transpired. "Jennifer implied that she would be acting as Phil's attorney and asked to tag along in the RCMP chopper. I had no way of verifying if she was or was not, so I conceded. What I can tell you is she wasn't working for us."

When Jennifer was finished, Phil summed up his feelings with, "I think we're done here." He got up and left.

He knew they could only convict them if they could prove the *Western Wind* was not flying a flag of origin. "The Coast Guard had removed our mammoth Canadian flag the day we docked in Port Angeles. That was step one in their process of deceit.

"The prosecution's plea, however, fell apart when Shawn's appointed lawyer presented to the court the short news video taken from a helicopter flying over our ship as I brought it into port and there as bright as day was our Canadian flag, flying proudly off the stern.

"Recognizing the feds were lying under oath, the judge threatened to charge them all with contempt and perjury. He took such behaviour personally in his court and wasted no time in throwing the case out. The only recourse left to them was to charge us with illegally entering the U.S. So, now we waited in the Immigration cells for our hearing.

"They call us the criminals. These very agencies, who are heralded as examples for the rest of us, lie, deceive, supplant evidence or remove it, just to ensure a conviction. And when they are caught, nothing happens to them."

To this point, the kid was the only one who had encountered Red. As they passed in the kitchen, Red shied away, making it painfully clear he had attempted to sell them out.

The day came when they were all herded into the same van and driven north on U.S. Hwy 5 towards the Canadian border. Red was with them but behaving as though he had been shot up with some kind of robust sedative. Phil lit into him: "Did you rat us out or what?"

"They asked me questions and I said nothing, cause, I don't know nothin," he responded while staring at the floor. Phil figured he was far from convincing. Shawn added his own two cents, but it was far less tactful than Phil.

Red raised his head. "They told me I would go to jail for the rest of my life and arrest my whole family too. I was so scared, I couldn't think. They yelled at me and I just couldn't take it anymore." The kid called him a "piece of scum" and that was the end of it.

CHAPTER 17

As they arrived at the Blaine, Washington border crossing, the van proceeded to the rear of the Canadian Customs building. Hordes of people were creating a ruckus as they pressed against the chain-link fence that separated the building from the U.S. side. Phil figured there had to be over 100 onlookers, plus helicopters circling on both the American and Canadian side.

The side door to the van opened and each crew member was manhandled out and shoved into a second van; except for Phil. He was held by the Americans, without cuffs, in the middle of the parking lot.

Pat Convey's partner, Dave Watt, walked over with a few American agents in tow. They were all wearing full body armour, bulletproof vests and carrying AR-16s. The van's escort personnel were still there, but their interest seemed to be focused on grabbing a final trophy photo of them handing over one of the world's most wanted international gangsters. That took all of ten to fifteen minutes.

When the photo shoot was over, Dave steered Phil's right elbow towards the gate in the chain-link fence. Phil figured beyond it lay Canada and, hopefully, freedom. On the far side, however, stood ten or so uniformed RCMP officers waiting patiently for him to step across the invisible line that separated the two countries. It only took a few minutes for him to realize his tribulations were far from over.

Dave ushered him into the back of a dark blue, unmarked van while two uniformed officers took up the front. In a rare act of kindness, Dave handed him a package of cigarettes and a lighter without even inquiring if he was interested.

It had been two weeks since he left the ship, prior to which he had a three-pack-a-day addiction. While in confinement, he had no choice but to go through withdrawal, leaving him uncertain now whether this was a good time to quit altogether or dive head long back into the habit.

Dave was quiet for a long while, but eventually he spoke. "Well Phil, what now?"

Phil knew they were heading east on Hwy 1 away from Vancouver, so an imminent release didn't appear to be in the cards.

With apparent tenacity in spades, Phil wondered if they'd ever give up.

"Well Dave, if you guys ever expect any help from me, you had better make certain my crew are sleeping in their own beds tonight." Following a quick call on his cell phone, Dave replied, "Yeah, I can make that happen."

"Okay, do it and have them call me when they are home."

Having gone down this road before, Phil knew the cops had forty-eight hours to prop him up in front of a judge or any attempt at a case would be an utter waste of time.

Well east of the Vancouver city limits, Dave handed Phil a blacked-out face mask and asked him to put it on. "This is for your own safety," is all he would say. Thirty minutes later, still blindfolded, he was led into a jail, the location of which was never disclosed. Dave said nothing but removed the blindfold and left the building.

As Phil was led down a narrow hallway with cells lining one side, Shawn's smiling face peeked back at him through one of the cell door windows. Phil was directed to the furthest cell from the main entrance.

It was late in the day, and he had received nothing in the way of food or drink since breakfast in Seattle. When the small viewing door to his cell opened, he expected to see something to satisfy his hunger, but instead, the officer who introduced him to his cell handed him a phone.

It was the kid on the other end, "Hi Skip, are you okay?"

"I'm good. Where are you?"

"I'm at home with my family. The police said I had to talk to you and let you know where I was."

As Phil began to ask if the kid would call Marlene and let her know what was happening, the line went dead. The phone rang again, but this time it was Red on the other end, the last person he had any interest in talking to.

Before the cop left, Phil asked if he was going to get fed. He also asked if the provision of a blanket and pillow to buffer the cold steel bed that had no mattress was out of the question. "I just do what I'm told, sir," was the cop's surly reply. Fifteen minutes later the guy returned with two McDonald's take-out bags containing a coffee, an Egg McMuffin, but no sugar, cream, or napkin.

The next morning, Phil was awakened by a different officer carrying a set of cuffs. Without a fuss, he got up, wiped his eyes, and extended his arms through the small access door so they could be applied. As he walked past Shawn's cell, he noticed the door was open and the cell was empty.

Shawn was standing beside Dave Watt at the top of the stairs leading into the main processing area. No cuffs and smiling. With no word as to where they were going or what was to follow, Dave removed Phil's cuffs and led them both out the front door and into the hands of five uniformed officers.

They were placed in the back of an unmarked car, with Dave and a driver up front. Before they had travelled more than a couple of blocks, Phil and Shawn recognized their location as Maple Ridge, forty-four kilometres east of Vancouver.

Denny's restaurant was their first stop, where Dave took over a table in the corner, large enough to seat all eight of them. A few minutes later, an additional four, much younger uniformed cops joined them. All were wearing Kevlar vests under white windbreakers.

Phil and Shawn accepted the government's generosity and ordered just about everything on the menu. Denny's is not known for its gourmet food, but to the duo, this was the best grub they had tasted since leaving the ship.

For once, the boys in blue were relaxed enough to allow Shawn a visit to the washroom without an escort. Attitudes had changed. While this was well received, it brought suspicion on what Watt's true intent could be. Thirty hours remained in the forty-eight-hour window and Phil knew the cops had to act fast or he and Shawn would walk without prosecution.

Before they were finished eating, Dave Watt had moved to another table where he and another man spoke on their cell phones in lowered voices. This went on for a half hour. When Dave returned, he had a look of uncertainty about him. "We're going to be taking you back to jail but we are trying to get something arranged that will offer better accommodation and food." Again Shawn shared his library of profanity, which Phil knew was not going to help matters.

Phil advised Dave that he was going outside for a smoke, with Shawn picking up the beat and following along. Surprisingly, none of the cops attempted to stop or follow them. This was their first opportunity to share the forty-eight-hour window together, with only twenty-nine hours remaining. Shawn mentioned that he had been approached by the van's driver, whom he referred to as Wolfman. "He wanted me to convince you to cooperate with them in exchange for promises of being well cared for. They told me if I am unable to keep you under control or if we try and take off, they will dump us in Wilkinson Road Jail and let us rot. They also said they will call the papers and tell them we are rats so that the general prison population will try to shank us."

"Is that all they said?" was Phil's reply.

"I told them I knew the Hells Angels were involved and could identify them if I saw their pictures."

"You what?"

"I didn't know what to do. They said they would charge me, my old lady and my brothers and mother if I didn't cooperate."

"When did this happen?" Phil asked.

"When we got in the van at the border and you were giving autographs. Wolfman was yelling at me and telling me I would die in jail. One of the big guys had me pinned by the throat and threw me against the van. I was scared and just wanted them to stop shoving me around. I'm so sorry."

This conversation didn't bode well with Phil. He had a haunting feeling that Shawn was on the verge of selling him out as well. Anything he said around Shawn from that point on had to be well thought out and detail free. Regardless of all that had happened, Shawn wanted to run. They were still outside, with the cops seated and paying them little to no attention. Shawn figured the two could outrun the cops wearing their bulky gear. He thought they could find a payphone to call their wives and arrange for lawyers to extract them.

Contrary to Shawn's impulse, Phil figured he'd like to play the game with Convey and Watts a little while longer and delay the inevitable long enough for the clock to run out, then they'd be home free.

Back on the road, with Dave and Wolfman holding down the front, they pulled off into a small strip mall where Dave returned with a brown bag containing a couple of cartons of smokes. Watt knew Shawn had never been a smoker, so Phil saw this as an attempt at reconciliation. With his three-pack a day habit becoming the norm once again, his former addiction was back in full force.

Next stop was a sleazy looking hotel a few miles west of the mall. Wolfman pulled in, shut off the ignition and sat there for what seemed like hours. For certain it was no Hilton with the neon lights of a strip club blinking a hundred yards up the road. The building wasn't run down but the parking lot was filthy with all sorts of seedy characters milling about.

Dave and Wolfman got out of the car as their supervisor, Phil Humphrey, drove up. The trio moved away so their voices wouldn't carry, then gestured for Phil and Shawn to join them. They were led in through the front door of the hotel with a warning not to speak to anyone or create a scene.

With officers front and behind, they were steered up a flight of stairs to the second floor, and down the hall which was lined with fifteen to twenty heavily armed cops. *They don't want us to create a scene?* Phil thought. It's a joke to have so much firepower just to manhandle two well-beaten smugglers. In his mind, smuggling two and a half tons of cocaine didn't warrant such a fuss. If they had only known I had brought in eight tons during the preceding months, they may have relaxed just a tad.

Both men were led to a room at the end of a hallway where four heavily armed guards stood waiting. Once in, the door slammed behind them. But before the echo had died, the door burst open. Dave Watt was standing mid-point in the entrance with his nostrils flared. In he stormed, straight to the phone sitting on the nightstand, where he proceeded to tear it from the wall as though it were an ill-gotten weapon. Without a word, he turned and marched right back out, slamming the door behind him.

With Phil and Shawn doing their best to refrain from laughter, in walked Dave again, still clutching the phone with its long connecting cable trailing behind. He said nothing. Staring the two down, he left, closing the door quietly this time. It reminded Shawn of the look on his father's face when he had been sent to his room so many times as a child.

The window in the room led onto a roof that covered the floor below. From it they could jump without serious injury. The temptation was there but the imaginary clock suggested staying the course may prove the wiser option. The accommodation was far superior to that of a jail cell and there was hope that before long the food would be more palatable as well.

Phil suspected the room was bugged and likely fitted with a camera, so he motioned to Shawn to curb any conversation. Knowing a couple of Mounties were standing outside their door, Shawn yelled, "Hey, we're hungry. Are you guys going to feed us or what?" This drew a response, "Food is on its way." Not letting it go, Shawn added, "Drinks too, and some beer."

The TV was on, so they turned to the news in hopes of seeing their faces paraded before the cameras at the border, but there was nothing. A couple of days had gone by and they were already old news.

A knock on the door indicated their food had arrived. Hamburgers and fries via room service, no less. It had to be the standard cop diet, next to donuts that is. But compared to the U.S. prison it was a feast.

Phil was pretty certain Shawn was missing his girlfriend, Charity. He was edgy as hell and needing a good fix like only she could provide. This made him unpredictable. If he could just keep it under control until this time tomorrow, he could satisfy his itch all he wanted. Or more correctly, all she wanted.

During the middle of the night Shawn did as Phil had expected. He climbed down off the balcony, ran off and made a call to his girlfriend from a payphone, then shimmied back up the hotel's exterior drainpipe hoping to re-enter their suite without being noticed. But no such luck.

Phil had awakened in the night and realized Shawn's bed was empty, the bathroom door was open and there was no distasteful noise coming from that darkened room. The window, however, was open and that spelled out the scenario that had, indeed, transpired. Not wanting to make it easy for Shawn or be woken up to the unwanted noise of him clamoring back in, he closed and locked the window.

Sure enough, there was a light tap on the outside of the window from his very nervous but satisfied roommate. Phil had half a mind to leave him out there but after a few moments he thought better of it.

With two and a half hours left on the clock there were three heavy knocks on their hotel door. In walked Pat Convey and Phil Humphrey with a dozen people trailing behind. Without a word, Shawn was ushered from the room.

Convey opened the conversation with, "Okay Phil, you are going to do exactly as I say or die in prison and I'm going to charge everyone you know in this world along with you. You're going to help these people and do anything they ask. This is your one and only warning, there won't be a second. Understand?"

Phil knew these words were not idle as Convey had used similar ones in 1999 when he'd levied a string of charges against his wife and brother who were completely innocent.

His brother was a commercial pilot. After being dragged through the mire of frivolous charges, his position with the airlines was in tatters. He was ordered to do drug tests, submit to all sorts of unwarranted scrutiny, and required to defend himself in a trial that was eventually tossed due to a lack of evidence.

With that, Pat turned and marched out the door as four of his team followed. The eight that remained, including Dave Watt and Wolfman, looked like they had been beaten by the school bully. Dave excused himself to the washroom while Wolfman left the room with three others. This left three officers still standing wearing looks on their faces like they were grappling with what to do next.

After a moment or two, one of the guys sat down at the small table parked against the wall. While pulling a bundle of papers from his briefcase he whispered in the ear of another suit. The guy with the paperwork finally opened up to the other two as they discussed the previous night's hockey game, ignoring Phil as though he was an inanimate object.

With nothing being directed at him, Phil got off the bed, turned the TV to CNN and dialed the volume up loud enough so everyone could hear. The tension about the room suddenly eased.

Dave leaned over and whispered something to the two guys at the table. It was clear the serious questions were about to begin. All Phil had to do was stall another hour and forty-five minutes, after which he could walk out the door a free man and they could do nothing about it.

Phil was invited to the table where the fellow with the paperwork asked him to confirm his mother and father's given names, where he grew up, his income and more; all useless questions with answers readily found in their own files. Just the same, he answered them politely, with the exception of the one pertaining to his income. "I'm not sure. I have accountants that I pay to handle that for me and my companies and I do not get involved in the details," he responded. His answers continued politely and at great length, while the clock silently ticked away in the back of his mind.

As the questions continued, Dave Watt relaxed on one of the two beds watching TV with his sidearm and vest lying beside him.

To be certain of the time, Phil grabbed the morning newspaper that had been slid under his door and excused himself to the bathroom. He locked the door behind him as he attempted to burn off the fifteen minutes remaining on the clock.

When sufficient time had elapsed, Phil got up with a much-improved sense of confidence. He left the can and walked back into the room where the others were patiently waiting. Watts remained on the bed engrossed in the TV.

Seeing it was 2 p.m. and no one had eaten, Phil suggested lunch was in order. Sarcastically, Dave tossed him a menu and told him to order room service. He was really hungry, so he ordered the most expensive meal on the menu, plus a few appetizers. Dave took the list without a word, opened the door, and walked out.

Since it seemed that no one felt it necessary to get Phil before a judge, he started to second guess his understanding of the law. Was it forty-eight hours or seventy-two? He resolved to wait and see how the game was going to play out. From there he might have a better idea as to what his options were.

The door to the room opened and two cops walked in with trays of food, a case of Coke and a bag of bulk ice. One announced he would be outside if they needed anything further.

After eating, Phil fell asleep while the others continued to huddle over their pile of questions. He woke at 8 p.m. to an empty room and Shawn on his balcony knocking on the window.

"What's up?" Phil asked.

"I just phoned home and the old lady says the cops are bringing her to see us tomorrow, along with your wife. I had told Wolfman earlier that I wanted my girlfriend here right now if they wanted any further help from me. I guess they took me seriously."

Come morning, Watt let himself into Phil's room. From his lack of personal hygiene and bloodshot eyes there was no question he'd had a rough night. It was no surprise, as Shawn and Phil had snuck out during the night and watched all eight of the cops through their window swigging back part bottles of whisky. Little wonder none of them had a clue the very two criminals they were supposed to be guarding came and went without raising an alarm.

"I have a surprise for you," says Watt.

Phil knew the answer before he asked, "What's that?"

"Pat Convey has made arrangements for your wife to join you. Do you need anything, smokes, deodorant, toothpaste, clothes? Make a list and I will be back in twenty minutes to collect it."

While Phil appreciated the offer, he felt like telling Convey to stuff it and stop coddling him. His purpose was to turn him into a rat, not a friend, so quit insulting his brain with these outlandish gestures.

At 4 p.m. sharp, Phil stared out his hotel window as an unmarked car approached the front of the hotel with his wife Marlene in the back. Behind her was a second vehicle delivering Charity to Shawn.

As Marlene came to the suite door, Dave Watt and two other cops were standing over her shoulder smiling as though they had done some great service. Dave closed the door with the words, "See ya later." As soon as the door closed the tears flowed. Not just from Marlene but from Phil as well. They were not tears of sadness, but rather of relief.

There was much to discuss, but assuming the room was bugged, they kept their conversation to family and Phil's well-being. Marlene mentioned the faculty of Beau's school were being protective of him and his cousin, Carson. She also mentioned that Phil's lawyer John Green had been attempting to reach Phil, but the cops were stonewalling him.

When Marlene was initially collected by the police, to be brought to see her husband, they seized her cell phone and house keys. The cell phone was easy to rationalize, but taking her keys left her wondering if the cops intended to do an unauthorized search of their home and property during her absence. Marlene mentioned that, because Ralph Harris had been unable to reach him during his final days at sea, he had contacted Marlene's brother-in-law Gary and told him Lea Sheppe was waiting with a crew on high-speed boats and automatic weapons while all were wearing their colours. It was their understanding the cocaine was to be offloaded at East Sooke's Cheanuh Marina. Why Ralph had contacted Gary, neither knew.

Gary also told Marlene that Ralph was choked at the bikers as they had promised him $2 million for setting up the deal, but reneged, giving him only a few hundred thousand, saying it was more than he deserved for a simple introduction.

Neither Phil nor Marlene could rationalize why Ralph had shared such sensitive information with Gary thereby getting him involved. His brother-in-law knew nothing about what Phil was doing prior to that point in time.

Ralph said he had attempted to convince Lea Sheppe to leave the First Nations marina as cops were monitoring their movements from a trailer parked on higher ground but Lea brushed him off and told him to get lost. Phil had no choice but to rethink Ralph or Lea might be the rat that brought this entire deck of cards tumbling down.

"If the club was ready to shaft Ralph out of his $2 million, how differently would they treat me? Ralph and I were entitled to share 20 per cent of the load or $17.5 million. They had killed in the past for a lot less," Phil explains.

Prior to setting sail, Phil had invested months tracking down each of the players and noting the location of their homes. Only a fool would not do this, and Phil was no fool. "If everyone is honest, it all works out. If they're not, well you can figure it out for yourself."

Phil knew that logic spun both ways as the club already had his home address. Such a ploy was commonly used by the club to maintain an individual's cooperation.

CHAPTER 18

Phil and Marlene talked through the night on matters that didn't involve the cops. On a personal level, they were out of pocket for the cost of bringing the *Western Wind* up to a seaworthy state. Phil had agreed to pay the lawyers who represented his crew and for certain, Revenue Canada would attempt to bleed whatever they could out of his withering hide, whether justified or not. In addition to all this, their relationships with neighbours and friends had been undermined.

The next morning, Dave Watt was at their door inviting them to breakfast in the hotel restaurant. The rules were laid out: stay at your respective tables, if you have to use the washroom an officer will escort you there and back. Again, he insisted, "This is for your own safety."

Seeing the cops eating steak with beer, Phil followed suit with two beers, a whisky, a ginger ale, plus a double vodka and tonic for Shawn. All courtesy of the taxpayer.

Back in their room, Phil closed the door without a word to the four cops who escorted them and while it would hardly stop them if they had a mind to come in, he latched the security chain.

Two more days passed without anything of significance transpiring between him and the cops. No questions, leading or misleading came his way. They continued to eat together in the restaurant but remained constrained in their movements and were separated in the evenings.

On the third morning Watts came to the Stirlings' room and announced Marlene was to pack her bags as she was heading home in thirty minutes. After she had left, Watts came to Phil's room and told him to pack, as he was leaving as well.

Once on the road, Phil questioned, "Where are we going?"

"I'm not sure yet, but somewhere else. I just work here."

The first thing that came to Phil's mind was Watt's concern over Marlene calling their lawyer John Green to let him know where Phil was being held captive. Not wanting lawyer interaction of any kind they were on the move.

Fifty miles to the east they pulled into a cheap motel that offered no phone or movie channel, just a small television with poor reception. It was so small it might well have been salvaged from a 1950s scrap yard. The only view out the single, non-opening window was a red brick wall twenty feet away. Outside his door were the same two cops.

The routine had become boring fast. The forty-eight-hour clock had long passed, and Phil was considering making a run for it, accepting whatever the fallout might be. But he decided to delay any action pending consultation with his lawyer.

Just as he regained some sense of peace, his door opened with ten cops filing in. The lead officer spread several images, mostly faces, onto the small table where the phone normally sat. Some he knew, most he didn't. The guy running the show started in.

"Do you know who this is?"

The first image was Ralph Harris. The cops already knew the connection, so what value would there be in lying. Nonetheless Phil replied, "Of course I know who that is, don't you?"

"I want you to tell me, do you know who that is?" the guy repeated.

"Why would I tell you anything about anything? Have we not been down this road already? If you have a proposition, let's hear it. If you are going to arrest me, just do it. Lawyers are all over you or you wouldn't be here with me in this God-forsaken hole. So, what exactly are you proposing?"

The lead guy looked at Phil, then to his colleagues who were spread across the room.

Keeping the ball in his court, Phil continued, "Just so there are no mistakes and I am not going to be accused later of misrepresenting myself, I want a lot more money. Like $2 million, understand? You are still going to have to buy all my assets which will include my businesses, homes, cars and everything else I own right down to the rubber duck in my bathtub, all at fair market value as determined by an independent appraiser.

"You are also going to give me an annual wage of $200,000 until I retire at 65, plus all the benefits, health, dental, pension and a $10 million life insurance policy in the name of my wife and child, payable upon my death. You must supply me with a vehicle until I am settled in my new life along with a new identity for not only myself but any member of my direct and indirect family who I feel is in need. This is not a negotiation. Any questions?"

Phil knew this made him look like he was ready to roll but he was reasonably confident they would never go for such terms when they had earlier passed on his lesser demands. Besides, in a pinch, this was the best he could come up with.

"Okay Phil, I know it's not very nice for you right now, but we need to get through some things here and now." He placed more images on the table. They were all photos of Phil talking to various bikers dating back over the preceding year and a half.

The photos included club members at the *Western Wind* just before it sailed out of Victoria, plus photos of members affiliated with the Nanaimo, Vancouver East End and Montreal chapters walking with Phil as he left a Vancouver restaurant. They even had one of Phil receiving the paper bag with $40,000 in it after being pulled from the trunk of a member's car. It held the money he used to put fuel in the ship. Phil remembered the day clearly, including the fact that the bikers' banker had been sitting in the car at the time, but none of the RCMP images included a clear enough shot of him.

The lead guy continued. "We don't need you to tell us everything as we already know the truth. We just wanted to see if you would tell us your version of the truth. You are of no value to us if you are going to lie.

"What we do need from you is your financial background. I want you to sign a release on your income tax, your family background etc. and your permission to gather that information. That's all I want, and we will be out of your hair in twenty minutes. As for your demands, that is above my pay grade."

Phil realized then that they'd been on to him long before he'd set sail. That doesn't eliminate any of those who could be the rat, but it does disqualify the Colombian captain's announcement over Channel 16.

Feeling the information they requested would not come back to bite him, Phil cooperated. It was all directed at himself and not towards the club. As promised the white-collar mob was gone in twenty minutes.

The night that followed was sleepless as Phil struggled to pull his thoughts together on how to bring this charade to an end.

The ninth morning came without Dave Watt barging through his door.

Breakfast and lunch came as usual. During the evening Phil asked one of the cops guarding the door where Dave was and was told, "We don't know, nor do we know when they will be back. You will just have to wait. We are just here to protect you and that's all we know."

The next three days came and went in the same manner. No Dave, no word, no anything.

The fourth morning marked Phil's thirteenth day in captivity. Phil flipped out, kicking the locked door and yelling to the outside. "Open the door, you prick, and let me out of here. I'm leaving right now."

"Settle down," was the only reply, followed by the door opening, with the two guards pushing their way in, followed by four others.

The gloves were off. Phil bolted for the door, with or without their permission. Three of the cops grabbed him and held him while two others slammed the door shut and physically blocked it.

"Calm down and speak to Dave," one of them said as he handed him a cell phone.

Before Dave could get a word out, Phil attacked, "I'm leaving, pal."

"What's wrong?" Dave replied.

"The fact that you have to ask shows me nothing is happening with you guys, so I'm leaving."

"You can't do that Phil or we will have to arrest you. Convey's orders."

"Show me the money and let's get on with it or arrest me because I am leaving either way."

Dave responded, "Give me until noon and I will have some answers for you. Try and leave now and I will have you arrested and maybe others as well. It's your call."

Phil didn't know if he was bluffing or not. "It's pretty hard to read a man's face over the phone. Either way I was not willing to risk my family being dragged through any more of this. They were innocent bystanders."

"Okay, noon," and Phil handed the phone back to the cop without waiting for a reply.

He thought, the love for your wife and family makes one vulnerable. Anyone who chooses this line of work should remain single.

Noon came and all Dave could offer was that he would make arrangements for his family to visit. "I am doing the best I can so please give me a chance."

Day fourteen found Dave at Phil's door smiling ear to ear. "We're bringing your wife and son to see you, along with your nephew, Carson. We are also going to move to a better hotel for the duration of the visit."

Within fifteen minutes they were parked in front of the Harrison Hot

Springs Hotel looking out across beautiful Harrison Lake. The hotel was expensive, as was the food in the restaurants, but there was no denying it was a hell of a lot better than jail or for that matter the motel they had just left.

Phil knew Carson and his own son had gone through hell at school. Phil's endeavours were not a secret and for certain it must have led to a whole lot of taunting. He had no idea how he was going to address them or for that matter how they would address him knowing that he was the talk of the town and not in a good way. It was impossible to come out of the initial visit with his kid smelling like a rose. If nothing else, the time would give him and Marlene a chance to discuss what they were going to do next and what the consequences might look like with that decision.

Dave Watt laid out the new and improvised rules. They could walk around outside, but under no circumstances were they to leave the hotel property. They could eat anything they wanted and charge it to their room, plus the boys would have their own room next door, with an adjoining door, if Phil and Marlene wished. He promised the cops would not intimidate or purposely alarm the boys. Lastly, they were not to use the payphones or that would bring an end to their little reunion.

Phil agreed to the terms, knowing that they may be subject to change.

As expected, their third-floor room was beautiful with breathtaking views across the lake and the mountains beyond. It was too high off the ground to have jumping as an option, and there was no roof midpoint to break their fall.

When Marlene and the family arrived, she was shown to their room and left with her husband for whatever uncomfortable moments were to follow. It had been more than three months since Phil had seen his son, so there was no question emotions would flow. But the kids seemed undaunted as they frolicked about like the resort was some kind of Disney holiday. To some relief, Phil discovered the boys were celebrities in their school with fellow students asking them about 'stuff'.

The boy's concerns were not 'Why' or 'What now', rather, they were "We're thirsty. Can we get drinks? Can we go in the lake?" In the end they settled for drinks, the pool, and the hot springs.

It didn't take long for the boys to pick out the cops sitting by the pool, making idle chatter with each other. There was a male and female but from the look of the female, she wanted to play the male role and was uncomfortable acting the part of a girlfriend or spouse.

Because he hadn't seen them for a few days, Phil assumed Shawn and his girlfriend were otherwise engaged or had been released to go home.

When Marlene had joined him in their room, she mentioned she had spoken to John Green's brother Jeff, as John was vacationing in Greece. Jeff was also a fine lawyer and he had confirmed for her that Phil was now at liberty to leave, as the cops had lost their ability to put an end to this silly charade.

Marlene managed to bring her SUV to the hotel but when the cops demanded she hand over the keys she proved her moxie by giving them the spare set.

While the Stirlings were tired of the power struggle, they still wanted to see how it played out. Besides, the Harrison was far from a hardship and with the feds picking up the tab, what could be better?

Shawn and Charity finally came up for air long enough to visit the pool. He had been at sea for so long he likely found it difficult to unwrap himself from all the carnal pleasures Charity provided. Not confident of Shawn's allegiances, Phil kept Jeff Green's comments to himself as well as their plans to escape. He would just have to figure it all out for himself.

Shawn shared that there was a big meeting scheduled at the hotel in the coming days and that the cops wanted his and Phil's involvement.

Following lunch in the hotel restaurant, Phil and his family retired to their room to watch a movie. The cops had neglected to remove the phone from the boys' room, so while the movie kept the boys occupied, he slipped next door to contact Jeff Green on his home number. He answered right away and asked how everything was going.

Phil detailed what had transpired over the preceding sixteen days; the way he had been kidnapped and moved from one dump motel to another, the promises and threats, the physical abuse by certain cops, only to be led to prestige hotels each time his family arrived. He also shared his fear of reprisal, not by the bikers, but by the cops against Marlene and his family if he didn't cooperate.

Jeff suggested a bold move, one the lawyer was confident was legal. "If you are able, you, Marlene and the boys should walk out the front door and keep going. They have kidnapped you which is a criminal act they will go down for, I can tell you that. They cannot charge you with anything. Just leave!"

"But Jeff, the cops have threatened to arrest Marlene and others. Now Ralph Harris has implicated my brother-in-law by calling him and asking him all kinds of things about me and the boat, asking him to contact me on his behalf. I don't want them to have to go through what I've now been through."

"Phil, I am going to contact a good friend of mine, Denis Murray. He's well versed on the police and the only lawyer I know of who has successfully sued the RCMP and got a judgment. I will ask his thoughts before we go any further. If he agrees with me, I will come today with an escort to get you and your family out of there. They won't arrest you or Marlene in front of me." Phil stated he would phone him back at 4 p.m. for an update.

That afternoon Phil and Marlene were summoned to a meeting while Shawn and Charity watched the boys. When they walked into the small meeting room on the main floor there were twenty cops with Pat Convey front and centre. Jennifer McCormick, the lawyer who had approached Phil on the RCMP's behalf while he was locked up in Seattle was also present.

They were shown seats next to Jennifer while Convey stood across the table. Wolfman and Humphrey also took up space. Convey remained standing, still wearing the same trench coat he never seemed to take off. "Listen Phil, I've told you before, we are not screwing around here for one more second with you and your tantrums. We brought you here at our expense so you could see your family but you are going to have to do exactly as we tell you."

Marlene cut in, "And what if he doesn't?"

"Well Miss Marlene, then I am going to make sure he rots in jail as he deserves and maybe you along with him."

Jennifer jumped in, "Pat, if I could speak for a second." But before she could go any further, Marlene was on the attack. "Yeah, what are you doing here, Jennifer?"

"The RCMP felt it would be a good idea if I were here to represent you on some of the issues. Pat wants some assurance that you both are going along with the plan and is trying to ensure that you understand the risk and what we, or excuse me, the RCMP are doing to protect you."

Convey took the floor for thirty minutes while attempting to drive home the threat the bikers represented if they knew where he was. If that wasn't enough, he made it known that whether Phil cooperated or not, he, Marlene and their family were targets and lucky to have him and his team watching over them. All twenty well-paid heads bobbed in unison to his words.

The meeting ended with Phil and Marlene agreeing to nothing. They just got up, turned for the door and walked out. Jennifer followed in close pursuit while attempting to hand them her card. "Take it easy, enjoy your stay and we will talk later," she suggested.

The two walked straight past her, out the lobby's front door and down to the beach, well beyond their mandatory limits of the hotel property. No one attempted to stop them. They sat on a log and spoke quietly about what had transpired, what their realistic future might look like and their possible options.

Back at the hotel, two cops were waiting when they arrived. Shawn was there and his demands for Chinese food lightened the tension and provided a timely distraction. Apparently, it was an acceptable request as the cops grabbed two more of their clones with all ten piling into an RCMP van and heading for town.

Following dinner, Phil split off to the left and across the street with Beau and Carson for ice cream, while Marlene, Charity and Shawn spun right and headed for the liquor store further down the road. The four cops stood dumbfounded as to who was going to follow who. When they finally figured it out, one took off after Phil while the other three did their best to catch up to Marlene and her crew. Seeing the cops make such a big deal out of something so small, finally gave Phil a reason to smile.

As they returned to the hotel, Watt instructed Marlene that her nephew Carson was to return home, and she was to make arrangements with her sister Debbie to pick him up at the ferry. She, Phil, and Beau were to remain. The Stirlings figured something big was coming down, they just didn't know what.

Before breakfast on Phil's seventeenth day, they were requested to pack their bags in preparation to leave. The bags were loaded into Marlene's SUV and driven by one of the officers, while Phil and his family were ushered into the back of an unmarked police vehicle.

An hour later they pulled into yet another one-star hotel just outside Langley, at the corner of Highways 1 and 10. Privacy was a foregone pleasure as they would now share a small two-bedroom with Beau while dining was limited to the McDonald's with a child's play centre across the street.

The following day yielded nothing, except by mid-afternoon Beau was bored and climbing the walls. All he wanted to do was go home where he could rejoin his lacrosse teammates. The night that followed was the longest in Phil's memory. He tossed and turned, then tossed and turned some more. By morning he'd had enough.

CHAPTER 19

On the nineteenth day, at 5 a.m., Phil and his family got up, showered, dressed, packed, and headed for the hotel's front door. They were going home come hell or high water. As they left their room, one of the two cops guarding their suite asked them where they thought they were going. "Home," was Phil's firm reply.

The two guys pursued them along the hall threatening arrest if they didn't stop. When that had no effect they said they would be calling Pat Convey. The fourth-floor elevator door took forever to open and by the time it did, the Stirlings watched as Dave Watt ran half-naked down the hall toward them. As much as Phil tried to push them back, Dave and the two other cops squeezed themselves into the elevator just as the door was closing.

When it opened into the lobby Dave attempted to block Phil and Marlene from leaving. Phil didn't have the use of his full weight for leverage since he had a firm grip on Beau's arm, but he did manage to wedge the larger of the suitcases between him and Dave, leaving just enough room for them to squeeze under Dave's extended arm. By then, Beau was visibly shaken.

The commotion had created quite a stir among the hotel patrons and workers, such that they all stopped and gawked at the unfolding circus-like scene. With as controlled a voice as possible, standing barefoot, his shirt unbuttoned to his midriff and his 9mm slung over his shoulder, Dave again attempted to convince Phil that he was going to be arrested and spend the rest of his life in jail.

"Then do it, just do it and quit threatening. If not, then we are out of here," Phil blurted out, loud enough for the entire floor to hear. The very commotion that Watt and Convey were trying to avoid was now in full swing for all the world to see and hear. Cell phones were up and pointed, recording every sound bite. This form of situational control was not taught at the academy.

Marlene clicked the SUV's door fob on her extra set of keys. Phil loaded their luggage in through the back hatch as Marlene checked the rear seat, to make sure Beau had buckled himself in. In unison they hit the automatic door lock with Watt yelling through Marlene's window that he was calling Convey. One of the other cops took up a position directly behind their SUV as though his physical size could stop a four-thousand-pound vehicle from moving back and out of its parking spot.

Telling Watt to step away from the car one last time, Phil put it into gear and drove off. Free at last. Phil drove as Marlene navigated from the passenger seat.

Pat Convey weighs in on Stirling's departure.

"Indeed, we kept him for a number of days, but he was never under arrest. It proved a fruitless effort on our part to nail the higher echelons of the deal, the likes of David Gilles, Louie, as the bikers' banker was known and Ralph Harris.

"His leaving was a mutual decision. We had done all we could to make a case out of the tattered evidence that was left, but Phil was just not going to cooperate. The entire time he was under our control we were watching those who wanted him dead. The only reason he was still alive was because we had him well-guarded and constantly on the move.

"All this bravado that Phil is spewing off about how we treated him is nothing more than BS. Someone had to be responsible for repaying the bikers for their loss and Phil was the only man in their sights."

As Phil and his family approached the outskirts of Vancouver, two cop cars appeared in Phil's rear view mirror. He was not running, as he believed himself to be a free man, no longer captive to the false prophesy that the cops had his safety at heart. He believed the bikers were not the threat, but the cops. Even if he wanted to run, it was impossible as Highway 1 westbound was gridlocked with commuters starting their day.

Reaching the Vancouver Island ferry felt like a major triumph, but behind them the same two cops remained in view. Once parked in the queue for loading, one of the cops approached Phil's car and offered him the lone piece of luggage that he had abandoned in the hotel elevator. He said nothing but handed it over and returned to his vehicle.

For the duration of the forty-five-minute drive from the ferry to their home in Metchosin, the cops trailed close behind. The moment Phil turned into their driveway, the escort turned off and vanished. Their orders were to offer protection until they reached home and that was all. They retraced their route to the ferry back to their home turf.

Marlene and Beau remained in the car as Phil looked over the property. He could see from where he stood that the barn door was closed with the latch twisted at the same angle he'd left it some months earlier. The grass had been uncut for the duration of his travels and offered no evidence of someone having pushed their way through it. As for the house, as best he could tell, it had not been disturbed.

He made up his mind to call John or Jeff Green at 2 p.m. to discuss his present situation. The two lawyers were rarely in their office before then. Before much time had passed, Phil could hear the thump, thump, thump of chopper blades moving in from the north. Sure enough, the tail shaft held the red, white and blue strip with the insignia of the RCMP stenciled boldly on the chopper.

It hovered above his back door long enough for Phil to recognize Pat Convey looking down. It was low enough for the down-thrust of the blades to lift the shingles on his barn roof. Without a second thought, Phil flipped him the bird and returned inside. At any moment he was expecting a flotilla of cop cars to tear up his driveway, but none came.

While Convey was hovering, Marlene reached John Green on the phone. "What's that noise?" was the first thing he asked. Phil gave him a report. "That's Convey with a few others sitting thirty feet above our back door in the RCMP chopper. They've been sitting there for eight minutes now scaring the hell out of our son and doing their best to rip the shingles off the roof of our house. There are no support vehicles coming up my driveway, so I don't know what the hell their motive is."

Jeff Green was angry and ready for action.

"I'm calling the Aviation Licensing Board as we speak, can you give me the aircraft number on the bottom?"

Once Jeff had the number he hung up, but his brother John remained on the line. Minutes later, Phil could see a debate transpiring between Convey and the pilot, following which the chopper lifted and flew off to the east. John closed off by requesting Phil's attendance at his office. He didn't want further discussion on a line that may be compromised.

Convey is adamant Phil's story was mere fantasy. "This is utter crap. We flew no chopper over his house that day, let alone hover over his house. It's just typical Stirling BS."

According to Phil, at 4 p.m. sharp that same day, a cop car did come up his driveway with two uniformed officers inside. "What can I do for you?" was Phil's opening line. "We want all your guns Mr. Stirling," was their reply. "You got a warrant?" was Phil's retort.

"Do you want us to go and get one and come back?"

Phil thought for a moment and decided he wasn't feeling up to additional trouble. "Do you want just the guns or all the bullets as well?"

"Our orders are to collect your registered guns, that's all."

While it may have been infringing on his rights, Phil didn't consider the request beyond reason. His neighbour had been required to forfeit his firearms for an impaired driving charge and that sentence hung over him for life.

Besides, it was only the registered weapons he was required to turn over. Most of his guns were not registered as he had ignored the 1995 federal gun registration law long enough that the bureaucrats eventually saw their stupidity and enforcement has been lax or non-existent.

Phil asked them to wait outside a second while he collected them. He had over a dozen hunting rifles and shotguns under lock and key. He removed the bolts, magazines, and scopes from those that were registered. If he was being forced to give them anything, he was determined to give them useless inoperative weapons at best.

When he was finished, he carried them to the back door and threw them on the ground in two heaps. He knew he would never see them again so there was no point in pretending they still held value. The cops picked them up one by one and left without a word. Besides, no one suggested he couldn't buy new ones.

He still had a number of handguns: .45s, 9mm and an Uzi with a silencer, plus a 50mm, a rocket launcher and a few hand grenades. But common sense ruled, they could never be registered.

When it came to these exotic weapons, Phil would say, "Mark my words, there will come a day when some foreign power will decide to take over our country and I for one will not give up my freedom without a fight. I will do all that I can to ensure my family survives."

Phil was awakened at 6:30 a.m. the following morning by a call from Dave Watt.

"Have you seen the *Seattle Times* this morning?" *How dumb*, Phil thought. *Like everyone on the planet gets the Seattle Times*. Just the same, he went to his computer and pulled it up. There in bold print was "Skipper Phil Stirling of the *Western Wind*, caught with 2,500 kilos of cocaine, said he used email while in transit to communicate with the Hells Angels."

"What a pack of lies. First the cops take away my guns so I'm unable to protect myself and my family, then they spread this kind of crap so the bikers will think I'm a rat and look for revenge. That's Canadian law enforcement for you. Leak a false story across the border so there's minimal blowback from their bosses. To them it would appear as though the U.S. forces were disgruntled and blowing off steam after bungling the seizure of the century."

The only source Mike Carter of the *Times* spoke of was 'confidential'. The article was spot on in suggesting Phil had been solicited by the RCMP to entrap the bikers. It was also true that he had come to know most of the large drug cartels in the world but the rest of it was utter trash. It was spun by those who wanted to force him into cooperating and couldn't make it happen without wrapping him in an envelope of fear. "These were dirty tactics spread by men who in my opinion abide by little to no ethical code."

The cops knew their opportunity to convict Phil and/or the bikers over the cocaine shipment had passed. They had a much better chance now of convicting the bikers of murder when they made their play on Phil's life. The cops didn't care how they scored a touchdown or who got hurt in the process as long as they saw their name in lights on the six o'clock news.

The article closed off by stating the DEA had seized his boat which would be sold as proceeds of crime while the cocaine would be sent out for incineration.

"In truth," Phil says, "Not much of the coke made it to the evidence locker and for certain none of it was destroyed. Some months later, a portion showed up in the hands of the Los Angeles Hells Angels, while the balance ended up with the Russian, just as it was intended.

"We know this to be a fact as our shipment was triple wrapped in duct tape and marked 'Azucar Sugar' to identify it as ours. Just keep in mind, no one or no government is going to burn $300 million in drugs, guns, or cash if it will benefit them in some way."

A week or two later Shawn connected with Phil, asking once again if he would consider working for the cops. "Why would I do that?" Phil responded.

"Because they are paying me and Charity $2,000 a month, plus they have us in a good hotel and are paying for our meals," Shawn replied.

Finally, one of Phil's questions had been answered. He was a rat.

CHAPTER 20

Knowing the cops would see them both as beaten and unlikely to cause further trouble, Ralph Harris went back to what he did best, importing without being troubled by the transport, while brokering local grow-ops, Phil Stirling, on the other hand, began plotting what his next move would be in the weeks immediately following his arrival home.

Phil made a call to El Chapo's lawyer, but not from his cell phone or from his home's landline as both were likely bugged. His brother-in-law lived a quarter mile away as the crow flies, so Phil made his way through the forest at the back of his property to Gary's place, then borrowed his car and drove to the nearest 7-Eleven where he purchased a new burner phone under a false name.

With the cultural formalities behind him, he asked if El Chapo would be kind enough to call him back at the new number as soon as possible. Ten minutes later the new phone rang. Joaquin rambled on for some time, extending an invitation for Phil and his family to move into a new home on his ranch in Mexico.

Phil finally had a chance to get a word in. "I need your help my friend. I need at least a ton of good pot. I will not have time to come ashore, so I will need it twenty miles offshore in the same spot as before. I will also be alone, so I will need a hand loading. I have only enough money for fuel so I will need credit, for which I will gladly give you forty per cent of the load's value when it is sold here in Canada. What do you say?" A deal was hatched.

With the boys thinking the nightmare surrounding the *Western Wind* was well behind them, Mike Carter from the *Seattle Times* walked through the Stirling's unlocked kitchen door, uninvited and unannounced, while Marlene stood in her nightgown fixing a coffee. Phil was away from the house hosting a client in his fishing charter business.

Straight away he lit into her demanding information about Phil and his dealings with the bikers. Even though she protested at the top of her lungs to get out of her house, he was relentless. It wasn't until the family Doberman reacted to her distress and came running from the master bedroom, that Carter decided a speedy exit was his best option.

Phil was with a client at the time so there wasn't much he could do and there was no use in calling the cops as they had likely put Carter up to it. But it didn't end there. Phil had to cancel his charter for the day, return the guy's $400 and race off to meet his family at a nearby McDonald's.

From the Stirling home Carter had made straight for Beau's school where he confronted the fourteen-year-old on the sidewalk in front of his schoolmates. Fortunately, one of the teachers saw what was happening and chased after the reporter, thinking he was a child molester, yelling that she had called the cops. The teacher took Beau back into the school where she phoned Marlene and the police, not necessarily in that order. As expected, the cops did nothing, making no effort to reach either Marlene or Phil.

The following morning Mike Carter wrote his second article. the bulk of which found its way into Julian Sher's book *The Road to Hell – Fishing for Cocaine with the Hells Angels.* The only difference between this and his first article was that he falsely professed this one was supported by an in-depth interview with Captain Phil.

Shortly after the Canadian Press article went to print, Ralph Harris called Phil to let him know that Lea Sheppe was shooting his mouth off about Phil being a rat and that trouble was soon to follow. As Ralph so often said, "He who hesitates dies," leaving Phil no option but to act.

Come daylight, Phil donned his armoured vest. He was going to solve this problem before it gained momentum or die trying. He grabbed his Desert Eagle 45 with six clips, plus his model 26 Smith & Wesson with two clips as backup.

The biker's clubhouse was approximately 100 kilometres north, or an hour and a half if he drove the limit. The clubhouse door was locked, so he knocked on it several times but no one answered. He then drove to Sheppe's house in Cedar. He could see Sheppe looking out the kitchen window so there was no question about him being home.

Sheppe opened with, "What do you want?"

Phil had his hand on his gun as he replied, "You got a big mouth pal. We're going to have a little talk or you're going to get popped right here and now." While Sheppe continued to push aside most of what Ralph had said, the conversation did lean in Phil's favour. Sheppe had never known Phil to pack a weapon, so in the end it was agreed he would spread no further rumours which could agitate club members.

CHAPTER 21

In mid-2005, British Columbia witnessed a weather system that dumped unheard of amounts of rain across the region. Few ma and pop marijuana grow-ops had the benefit of indoor facilities so their plants rotted or formed blights from the excessive humidity before they could be harvested.

The lack of home-grown product placed an enormous burden on the larger indoor illegal operations. They couldn't meet the demand. While B.C. bud remained the crème de la crème on a global scale, the market was starving for any form of saleable product.

A member of the Sherbrooke, Quebec chapter of the Hells Angels reached out to Ralph Harris and suggested that he could help alleviate the problem. This same fellow knew of the fiasco surrounding the *Western Wind*, but just the same felt that Ralph was a man he could trust.

The Angel wanted to know if Ralph would import 300 tons of Mexican marijuana to the Pacific Northwest. Again, it was not something Ralph had the ability to pull off on his own but knew Phil Stirling was always open for business.

What he didn't know was whether the apparent rift between him and Stirling had healed over the preceding year or whether the old wounds still festered. Whichever the case, if the job moved forward, he was determined not to be pushed to the sidelines like before.

Today, Phil questions his judgment at having entertained a second venture with Ralph, but his need for that rush of adrenaline that comes only from a mission such as this overpowered any form of common sense.

Phil had remained on a first name basis with Joaquin Guzman, a.k.a. El Chapo, of the Sinaloa Cartel, but contact with his old friend had become somewhat complicated since they last met. Guzman had been arrested in 1993 while working in Guatemala. He escaped in 2001 after paying a few prison guards a modest bribe, which led to the back door of the prison being carelessly left open. He was recaptured and then escaped a second time through a tunnel his boys had dug from the surrounding residential buildings into his cell.

Guzman's flight to places unknown, led to the U.S. placing a $8.8 million bounty on his head for any information leading to his capture. He was recaptured in 2016 and extradited to the U.S. in 2019 where he now serves a life sentence in Florence, Colorado. While this may have been viewed as an obstacle to anyone else, Phil's personal Rolodex also held a list of all those who knew how to reach him.

A load of 165 bales or 1,600 kilos was prearranged within a matter of days. Ralph's only concern was, "While Mexican pot is cheap compared to B.C. bud, it may look the same, but it smells like skunk. As they say, you only get what you pay for.

"One downside to the Mexican product is their TC content runs only 7 per cent to 8 per cent while the Canadian equivalent is 26 per cent to 36 per cent. This is no small factor in the minds of users who know the difference." Being a man who strived to maintain solid connections, Phil offered El Chapo 100 of Ralph's Canadian plants which he would bring on his trip south. This he could cross pollinate with his own stock and hopefully improve the Mexican strain.

"We agreed to pay US$90 a kilo for what would sell on any Canadian street, any day of the week, for $1,800 a kilo. As was the norm, we had to pay the Mexican Federales an additional $500 a kilo to truck the pot from the mountains to the coast."

The U.S. had not returned the *Western Wind*, so they were left with no choice but to procure a new ship. "Without a bankroll to complete the purchase we struck an agreement with the Mexicans to carry the deal until it could be sold."

Within a matter of weeks, Phil located the *MV Bakur* in a Halifax paper. It was 47 metres, 354 ton, built in 1961 with its primary use listed as a longliner for tuna fishing. It had a freezer unit on board, a satellite phone and a few other bells and whistles to aid in navigation. Age wise it was a little long in the tooth. Nevertheless, they felt it would serve their purpose.

The *MV Bakur* was purchased and registered as the sole asset of Limar Fishing Company with Phil, Ralph and Phil's son Beau as equal partners. "You don't need to know what we paid for the ship," Ralph said, "but I will tell you it was listed for $1.4 million.

"While ownership is equal, there is no financial equality in the deal. It was primarily my money that made the venture possible. If you have difficulty accepting that fact, check out my investment as per the director share agreement or the two mortgages on my Ladysmith home totalling over $500,000 that had been registered by Phil's wife Marlene during my absence.

"Each mortgage was commissioned by her as my power of attorney while I was en route with the *Baku*r and unable to do anything about it. Phil's primary contribution came in the form of his uncanny ability to find his way from Asia across the Atlantic to South America and then home to the Pacific Northwest without the need of charts or GPS."

Ralph and Ed Corbin packed Ralph's truck with their fishing gear and all they would need while away, then made their way east across Canada. In the meantime, Phil and Shawn Cochrane flew to the east coast to consummate the deal.

Corbin and Cochrane were the same two guys who helped out aboard the *Western Wind* during the trip to South America and back. While Shawn had proven himself to be a rat, the wounds between he and Phil must have healed sufficiently that Phil was now prepared to risk his involvement once again.

After an introduction to the workings of the ship, they moved it to a small Halifax shipyard that was begging for work and there they installed a false ceiling in the hold and a phony bulkhead forward of the same area. They paid the owner well and gave him a substantial bonus to forget he had ever seen them.

Not long after Ralph had arrived in Nova Scotia, he returned home to get some personal business dealings in order. A year earlier, during November of 2004, his grow-op had been busted but charges went nowhere. Restarting the operation was a no-brainer but any absence longer than a few days could render his harvest a complete loss.

Jillian Taker had not only been one of Ralph's many playmates, she also worked with him on a number of his ventures.

"In 2002 I had a heart attack during the early hours of the morning," Ralph recalled. "It was one of those rare occasions when I was actually alone at the house so I had to crawl down the stairs from the upper level, drag myself out to my truck and make my way over to Kathy's.

"The first thing she did was pump me full of baby aspirin before calling 911. If it wasn't for her, I would not have survived the day. The paramedics hauled me off to the Nanaimo hospital where they got me stable and then drove me to the Jubilee Hospital in Victoria where they do all the major heart surgeries. There they replaced five valves using veins from my legs and arms. I believe they referred to it as a quintuple bypass. I was a royal mess, so I was forced to stay there an additional five days.

"Meanwhile Jillian was supposed to be looking after my plants. The work isn't rocket science. All she had to do was drive over to my place once a day to make certain the plants had been watered by the automated system, had received enough nutrients and that the lights were still on.

"It's all pretty simple, but she managed to muck things up real good. A good crop was worth anywhere from $70,000 to $160,000 depending on whether I sold at wholesale or street prices. When I was released, the first thing I did was drive to my place and look in on them. As soon as I entered my barn I could smell the mildew in the air and see the plants were stressed beyond salvation. She had not done as she agreed and certainly never watered them as frequently as needed.

"The entire crop, plus all the juveniles ready for my next rotation were lost. The dollar value was beyond reason.

"If she hadn't been such an enjoyable person outside of work, I could quite easily have wrapped my fingers around her slender little neck and squeezed until there was no life left in her. I had done far more to a few others for a lot less."

CHAPTER 22

While Sgt. Wayne Flewelling was investigating the *Western Wind* fiasco as it pertained to Phil Stirling and his crew being hung out to dry as informants, Phil unwittingly told Flewelling that he was purchasing the *MV Bakur* to go fishing.

"I was working with the RCMP Internal Affairs Department when my investigation began. Phil's background as a consummate smuggler could not be ignored so I found his suggestion of a pending fishing trip rather suspicious," Flewelling explained.

Following his gut feeling, Flewelling passed his thoughts up the line to members who considered the interception of contraband part of their daily routine.

"One thing led to another, with our counterpart in Halifax paying the Halifax Harbour a visit and taking a good look at the ship. The RCMP remained there for a few days to confirm Phil's involvement in its preparation. Stirling, in the company of Shawn Cochrane, flew in during the evening of November 10 and was greeted at the ship by an unidentified character that appeared to be residing on board. Ralph Harris arrived with Ed Corbin a few days later in a pickup truck loaded with fishing gear.

"From there the *Bakur* investigation became officially known as 'The E-Penny Operation'.

"From November 20, 2005 forward, daily surveillance of the *Bakur* and the movements of all those on board were recorded. From past experience, we were pretty certain his intent was to use the fishing trip as a decoy, when he really intended to bring another load of drugs into the country.

"On November 21, we secured a warrant to install a tracking device on board. Due to the number of bodies coming and going, we were unable to install it until December 22 which was none too soon as the ship sailed clear of Canadian waters on the 31st."

Before they set sail, Ralph and Phil added four local boys to their crew's manifest: Joe Munden, Robert Forsey, Winston Childs and Rene Slaney.

The cops wanted every advantage, so they asked for and received a warrant to monitor Phil's satellite phone.

Heading south along the U.S. east coast, the ship stopped in Miami to take on 16,900 gallons of fuel. From there they fished across the Gulf of Mexico, after which they sold their catch to the Mexicans for $360,000. "We hid the money behind our false bulkhead to avoid having to explain its source, if we were stopped," Ralph explained.

Their stop at Port of Spain, Trinidad on January 13 turned sour as the four Newfie members jumped ship. According to Phil, "They tried to convince the balance of our crew to mutiny as well but they struck out.

"Dumb as a bundle of dry sticks, they fled, leaving their passports and personal property behind. After they failed at trying to extort Ralph and me for what they believed was their entitlement to the catch, plus a plane ride home, they had no choice but to resort to the Canadian Embassy for aid. In turn, we had no option but to continue short-staffed until we reached Panama where we were able to hire replacements."

Whether it was wise or not, both Shawn Cochrane and Ed Corbin emailed Wayne Flewelling of the RCMP on January 19, 2006 to report Joseph Munden, Rene Slaney, Winston Childs and Robert Forsey, had attempted to extort money from them. One thing is certain; if the RCMP had lacked confidence in their on-board tracker, they now knew with certainty where Ralph and his crew were.

From Panama they sailed north to Altamar, Costa Rica before turning south once again and into the Panama Canal. Ralph explained, "If we were going to continue fishing, we needed the extra manpower. Once our fishing equipment was packed away for good, we took them to port and paid for their flight home."

"It took $40,000 in fees, plus a number of days for the lineup of ships to clear the Panama Channel and allow us to head north into the Gulf of California where we were to collect our 1,600 kilos," Phil recalls of the voyage. "Our pickup point was Topolobampo, northern Sinaloa, Mexico, approximately 14 miles southwest of Los Mochis, that being the home of my good friend El Chapo."

As soon as the RCMP tracker indicated their destination, the cops had no doubt as to the trip's intended purpose. That port had become well known for its infamous resident and his product of choice.

"The day following our arrival, a representative of the Sonora cartel drove Ralph and me into the hills to show off their crop and the method they were using to harvest the bud," Phil recalls.

"Anyone who smokes the stuff knows the flower of the plant provides a superior high to the leaves. The Mexicans have done wonders to improve their product over the past few years, but it still doesn't compare to what we were producing back home."

Not long after they arrived in Mexico, Ralph announced he had to fly home for the funeral of a family member. According to Ralph's daughter, "He came home to get some money to pay for the ship's fuel, as both he and Phil were tapped."

Ralph explained the trip back to Vancouver Island may have been inconvenient but it was essential to the mission's success.

"I flew home from the 24th of March until the 13th of April which was a long time with the crew itching to get underway with our load, but it was unavoidable.

For the remainder of their stay, they spent the majority of their time in Los Mochis under El Chapo's protection. No bandits, Federales or opportunists would consider messing with them."

The RCMP stood ready for Ralph as he stepped off his flight. A team of four officers in two cars tag-teamed him from the moment he left his property each morning, until he returned in the evening.

According to the RCMP report: "He did nothing overtly criminal, but unquestionably odd. On one day he drove to two different Royal Banks, one in Ladysmith and then an hour later, the main branch in Victoria. During this same expedition he stopped at the Tempo self-serve fuel station at the corner of Hwy 1 and Mt. Sicker Road. That is not in itself unusual, but as soon as the proprietor saw him pull up, he came out from behind the till to pump the gas into Ralph's vehicle while the two spoke.

"Oddities didn't end there. He stopped at the A&W in Mill Bay, followed by the White Spot on Douglas Street in Victoria, then Serious Coffee in Mill Bay on his return, followed by the Cow Bay Pub, the Spice Shack and the Good Company Steak House, both in Duncan before returning home."

The cops couldn't help but wonder how much one man could drink or eat during the one-hour drive home.

The fact that he was driving his daughter's light blue '96 GMC Blazer, meant little. The unidentified female companion, who was estimated to be in her twenties, with shoulder length brown hair, and who wasn't his daughter, again offered nothing to justify the RCMP's deployment of manpower.

Back in Mexico, Phil stewed over his partner's time away.

"Ralph's absence was troublesome, but as it stood, the load wasn't ready when we arrived. Each bale had to be wrapped repeatedly, layer upon layer in commercial plastic wrap until the wrapping was about half an inch thick. The Mexicans placed (anti-static) sheets between each layer, swearing it would throw off the drug dogs. Over this would go the outer burlap wrap, followed by duct tape around and around until it was secure. Markings identifying the source of the dope and its buyer were stamped to the top of each bale. If any went astray and was found by another, this would permit a ray of hope at knowing who it belonged to."

During this down time, Phil and the crew devoured the town for over two weeks getting drunk and tasting every woman they could hold onto. It was all-out partying. The cartel is not shy about using lethal force, but in the case of the *Bakur* they employed a couple of the off-duty Federales to patrol the wharf and discourage curiosity seekers from straying too close.

When the load was ready, the ship was moved twelve miles offshore, away from prying eyes and the 300 tons of pot was brought on board.

"Once El Chapo was paid in part, we purchased fresh groceries sufficient to carry us home and paid the Federal Police Commandant the $500 per kilo owed to transport our load from the mountains to our ship."

In the dead of night 142 bales were stuffed above the false ceiling and another 23 behind the new bulkhead. Everything flowed without a hitch.

Because the transaction required a measure of credit, El Chapo insisted Ralph and Phil take one of his people, Walberto Armenta-Ruelas, on board as a deckhand for the return trip. He wasn't a kid and based on his appearance he would be in his early forties. His comfort level with the ship's movement made it clear he had been down this route before and was prepared to ensure nothing went wrong with their end of the deal and if it did, he would deal with it. The guy didn't have a passport and it was likely his rap sheet would have rendered him ineligible had he tried to get one. Regardless, as long as he remained on board, he didn't need one.

Feeling rather smug with $6.5 million retail in pot below deck, Ralph and Phil headed for home. As luck would have it, the engine started giving them problems off the coast of California while cruising deep within international waters.

"We knew if we stayed well clear of their legal limits, the U.S. DEA or Customs would have no authority to intercept and board us for a routine drug search, but all that changed when we were forced to radio for assistance." A radio dispatcher in San Francisco responded and based on the questions they asked, Ralph and Phil knew their call for help had raised a red flag with the DEA and Customs. Within the hour a U.S. Customs ship was bearing down on them at what appeared to be full throttle.

"We had no doubt they were determined to intercept and board us. As it was, they fell in behind the *Bakur* and held our course as we limped into San Francisco Bay where repairs could be made," Ralph recalled.

"As soon as we tied up to the government wharf a handful of well-armed cowboys from the U.S. Customs invited themselves on board to have a look around. They completed what we thought was a fairly comprehensive inspection but for one reason or another they never commented on the new metal work or fresh paint. I found this a little hard to believe as every corner of the ship stunk from a toxic mixture of urethane paint and the weed which had been sealed in the hold without ventilation for a number of days," Phil says.

When the inspection was over, an officer with the San Francisco's customs office, identifying himself as Mark Shelley, came on board bearing pizzas. They hadn't thought it was going to be a social call, but the guy wasted little time in asking if they were willing to bring a load of cocaine in from South America for his agency.

"Something in my gut told me it wasn't part of a sting but rather another CIA sponsored type of drugs for arms affair, so we didn't say yes or no, but rather we would have to get back to him once this trip was behind us," Phil explains.

Ralph learned later that the U.S. Customs had contacted the RCMP in Victoria with a courtesy request which would allow them to board the *Bakur* while the ship was in international waters. The RCMP told them they had everything under control, so they asked them politely to stand down. Their monitoring of the onboard tracker had indicated an abrupt diversion from their course north into American waters, so they were not surprised when they received the request.

Pressing forward after repairs were made, Ralph and Phil felt their best option was to continue north up the west coast of Vancouver Island to the Ucluelet Harbour. As backup surveillance, the RCMP sequestered an Aurora aircraft out of Comox Air Force Base to fly south once the ship was within range. There the RCMP had an opportunity to confirm the ship's progress and take supportive photographs.

"We had narrowed all their possible docking sites down within the region and mobilized teams ready to react on a moment's notice," reported Const. Allen of the Ucluelet detachment. "On the 21st at 7:41 p.m. our tracker stopped working, so we had no idea whether they were heading into Ucluelet or points further north."

A day later, in the dead of night, the *Bakur* slipped into the Ucluelet harbour. Ralph and Phil both felt something wasn't right, though they were uncertain as to what it was.

"Our ship's radar was blinking with far too many dots showing small watercraft moving about on the surface of the harbour, especially for two in the morning," notes Phil. "Our intent was to tie up at the '52 Step Marina' for the remainder of the night and then offload at the fish plant in the morning. The bales of weed had already been packed away into large commercial fish crates. We would just roll up to the plant the following morning and offload in broad daylight with no one the wiser."

At 2:20 a.m. they pulled up to the '52 Step Marina' wharf but a smaller fish boat, approximately thirty feet in length was tied up in such a way that it blocked the larger *Bakur* from gaining enough wharf to secure itself.

There seemed to be no life on board the smaller craft, so Ralph with one other fellow leapt from the bow of the *Bakur*, untied the smaller boat and pulled it forward, while Phil nudged their ship in tight.

No sooner had the small fish boat been secured, Fisheries officer Michael Crottey in the company of Customs officer Klassen, invited themselves on board.

Crottey reported, "A male in his 40s to 50s, wearing a grey Stanfield, introduced himself as Stirling, the skipper. I told him I was there to complete an inspection, to which he stated he had tuna and did I wish to see them?

"I introduced the Customs inspector and suggested he would be completing an inspection as well. At that point I asked Stirling if he would bring all those on board forward to the galley. After everyone was gathered, I explained what was happening while Klassen went forward to confirm all were present."

With formalities out of the way, Crottey proceeded outside to inspect the catch. The hatch was removed from the hold forward of the wheelhouse to reveal expandable foam sealing the entrance. Beneath the foam lay rope and ground lines of various colours.

"As the ropes were pulled aside, packages wrapped in tape were exposed. One package was slit with a pocketknife to reveal a strong 'skunk cabbage' smell.

"When the forward hatch in the bow port side was opened it appeared empty. The forward starboard hatch however held bait fish and about 20 tuna in poor condition. They were not frozen as water was mixed with blood beneath them."

Without showing alarm, Crottey returned to the wheelhouse where he asked Stirling for his logbook and license, then directed them to proceed out onto the main deck.

Within seconds, four high-speed, rigid hulled inflatables charged the *Bakur* from all directions, each loaded with heavily armed RCMP in full combat dress.

After Ralph had secured the small boat, he sensed something was not right and hid between the wharf pilings. He could hear the cops demanding that Phil and his crew lay prone on the salt encrusted deck.

"There were no jihadists around but that didn't stop the cops from turning up in ninja gear with every gun they had in their arsenal," Ralph would say later.

"The number of craft and the size of the force pitted against us was an absolute joke. The same results could have been achieved with the use of a single watercraft and maybe a half dozen wet-nosed constables. Like what were we going to do? Turn our 154 ft. ship 180 degrees and race out of the harbour at Mach 1? This was not our first dance, so the authorities knew we weren't the kind to grandstand and go out with guns blazing. Those days were lost decades ago in the TV westerns.

"If I headed back to the *Bakur* I knew my fate was sealed, so I moved further down the wharf towards the stairs that led to dry land, just as two more cops came out of the cabin of the small boat I had just moved. Dumber than a load of bricks, they had neither seen me, nor realized their boat had been moved. Their eyes were locked on the *Bakur* so I just slid back in behind a couple of pilings and waited for them to move into the shadows," Ralph recalled of his bold attempt at escape.

As they reached the *Bakur,* Ralph made his way to the base of the steps. While it was an impossible course to navigate without detection, it was the only route Ralph could see.

"As soon as I reached the base of the steps, two more guys started coming down with flashlights, backpacks, and each restraining a dog on a leash. It didn't take a genius to figure they were part of our welcoming party, so I slid back in behind some other pilings until they passed.

"When the four had boarded the *Bakur*, I made for the stairs once again, but halfway up I was interrupted again by another two guys at the top. With less than a second to consider my options, I leapt over the side of the steps and onto the rocks below while moving sideways into the shadows beneath the steps.

"Fortunately, the tide was out, otherwise I would have made quite a splash and been left treading water as they fished me out. From below I could see the beam of their flashlights progressing downward through the slats in the planking above me. As soon as they had cleared the immediate area, I abandoned the idea of using the stairs and crawled hand-over-hand up the steep embankment, then picked my way north through the rear yards of the residential properties that fronted the marina. I figured if I could move far enough, they may just pack up their troops and leave me be.

"I don't know how far I thought I was going to get, but I can tell you it didn't end up being far at all. A hundred meters along Imperial Land, I walked straight into a half dozen cops who seemed more than curious as to what a single, disheveled man would be doing making haste out of the area in the wee hours of the morning. As it ended up, they were more than happy to offer me a ride to the Ucluelet detachment.

"If I had my wits about me, I may have had better luck hiding under or behind one of the houses lining the waterfront for as long as it took for the heat to die down. Or, if luck would have it, I would have tripped across my girlfriend Joanne who I had prearranged to pick me up."

With the four remaining crew clustered together, they were read their rights and asked if they understood. For the Mexican crew member, the caution was translated by one of the cops who spoke Spanish. Stirling identified himself as the captain and owner of the ship and was then asked if he had anything to say. "I wish to remain silent," was his only reply.

Ralph explained: "The boys we had lined up to help with offloading had seen the cops milling about the wharf long before our arrival, so they hightailed it out of there rather than find themselves embroiled in what was to come. They had no way of reaching us, but even if they had, we would never have been able to outrun the well-equipped flotilla of assault boats. Besides, there was no place for us to go."

Stirling and Corbin were escorted into one of the patrol cars, while Amenta, Ruelas and Cochrane were ushered into another. Each was asked if they wanted to call their lawyers. Stirling replied, "I will get one for all of us." Cochrane responded, "I don't have one to call at 3 a.m."

They were asked as a group if there was anybody else on the ship. They all responded, "Ralphie is the only other person, and he should be out there somewhere." If the cops had no knowledge of Ralph's involvement prior to that moment, this group of less than loyal shipmates sealed his fate.

Const. Allen adds, "We knew he was on the loose and while he wore a dark jacket, his bright orange ball cap shone like a beacon as soon as he came out of the shadows."

At this point they were all informed they were under arrest and what the charges would be, after which they were photographed, fingerprinted and placed in separate cells. The Mexican was removed from his cell, interviewed by an Immigrations officer and charged with illegally entering Canada.

When asked why he had come to Canada without a passport or without speaking to anyone from Immigration, he responded, "I came to work for the man on the boat fishing tuna so I could support my child." When asked who introduced him to the captain of the ship, he replied "Francisco Gasterum". When asked if the drugs were on board at that time, "There was nothing when I got on, they were loaded a day later in the middle of the night out in the open sea. I asked the captain to let me off the boat, but he said no. I could see them loading the bales but I didn't help." When asked if he wished to speak with someone from the Mexican consulate, he replied "Yes."

At 3:45 a.m. Stirling called the guard asking for permission to call his lawyer. He was shown a phone in the interview room which was set on speaker phone. The officer present could hear, "This is the voice mail of John Green." The officer then left the room so Phil could speak in private. Within the hour, everyone had lawyered up.

Inspector Paul Nadeau of the Greater Vancouver Drug Section identified himself as the officer in charge. He refused to comment to the press other than to say the RCMP had been tracking the ship's movements since October 2005, well before the December date when they sailed clear of Halifax Harbour.

Nadeau also informed Ralph and Phil that the *Bakur* was to be towed the following day to the Naval yards in Victoria where cops would literally tear their ship apart from front to back as part of their investigation.

Hamming it up for the evening news, Nadeau puffed up his chest as a Ucluelet reporter asked what the RCMP had found. "Clearly, when you use a vessel of this size, you're going to be talking large quantities. It could take quite a while, so I won't speculate as to how much is on board. But you know it's a fairly sophisticated operation when you're resorting to this mode of transportation and you're travelling those sorts of distances. We're expecting it to be a fairly large amount of drugs."

As best the cops could tell, there seemed a large quantity of pot stuffed in confined spaces where air quality would be poor and breathing apparatus may be required to access safely. It was decided that any attempt at removing the cargo should wait until the ship was moved to a more suitable location.

The ship's engines continued to run following the removal of the crew as the cops lacked any understanding as to how they could be shut off.

When Shawn Cochrane had left the ship, he had made it known that he had retrofitted the engines to keep them running. "If you shut them down, the ballast pumps will not be able to keep it afloat and it will sink." Nadeau summoned an RCMP marine engineer to confirm the vessel was seaworthy. As scheduled, the *Bakur* was taken under tow by a Seaspan tug at 8:30 a.m. the following morning with four officers on board to secure the evidence. They made straight out of the Ucluelet harbour into the rough waters of the open Pacific.

At precisely 9:45 p.m., the ship was secured to the DND Navy D1 Jetty on Wilfert Road in the District of Colwood, 11 kilometres west of Victoria.

A trailer was brought in to serve as a mobile command centre so the cops had a place to enjoy a little R & R when needed. It was estimated the search portion of the seizure would take two or more days with Canadian Border Services Agency taking the lead role. Two officers were brought in on May 23 to photograph and video the search to play a part in future training and media presentations.

An assortment of electronics was seized from the ship, all of which were passed along to RCMP technicians for the purpose of gleaning radio frequencies that had been used on the vessel, historical records as to the vessel's positioning during its travel, records of all incoming and outgoing telephone/cell satellite phone calls.

Privacy today is not so sacrosanct as it was back in the '70s, or '80s. Today's federal investigator can eavesdrop on your cell calls or emails. They can hack in through your computer's backdoor, or any other electronic device for that matter, and read firsthand every message you've sent, even those that you think have deleted, plus they can digitally visit every site that you visited. If you own a vehicle newer than the '80s it is likely the cops can download off the vehicle's onboard computer where you have been at any given time of day. Hence the motto of the day is if you are going to do something that will alter someone else's life, don't use your own vehicle, steal one temporarily.

Unless you are tech savvy or make the determination never to leave an electronic footprint that could turn into evidence, your defense mechanism will be all but gone when the cops come knocking on your door.

The following day, Fisheries officer Richard Christiansen came onboard with instructions to inspect the estimated 5,000 pounds of tuna and mackerel stored in the forward freezer. After taking a number of photographs, he reported, "It is my opinion the tuna and mackerel were not food quality. The freezer floor was wet and there was no coldness in the freezer. That would indicate it had not been operating in recent days. A decaying fish odour was present in the air."

Christiansen contacted Dave Davidson of Island Processing to see if he would purchase the load for reduction. He replied that he didn't pick up fish but if they were transported to Nanaimo he would look at them to see if they were suitable for reduction. Based on the description provided by Christiansen, he felt they would be best suited for delivery to a local landfill. Christiansen also contacted Richard Strong of The Fish Store in Victoria but Strong replied he was not interested and knew of no one who would be.

Supporting Christiansen were Fisheries officers detailed to inspect each fish to ensure no contraband was concealed inside.

At 11:35 a.m. on May 25, Tom Whyte of Intercon Marine removed the fish to the Hartland Landfill where the seagulls, crows and wildlife would have a feast.

Marine Engineer Norm Bennett was engaged by the RCMP to survey the vessel. In his report he noted what appeared to be new concrete in the forward fish hold, plus a number of areas of new construction and the fact that the ship was listing heavily to the port side, a situation he wished to explore further. With the report in hand, holes were drilled into the chain locker and elsewhere to provide access for a fiber optic scope, while the concrete within the fish hold was jack hammered away.

In support of Bennett's report, a remote oceangoing vessel was deployed to examine that portion of the hull underwater for the possible placement of limpets, the acronym for exterior attached concealment devices.

On May 24, 143 bales, each measuring 14" x 11" x 12" were extracted from the forward and rear fish holds. Another 16 were recovered from the area behind a front wall of the vessel and a further six were pulled from cupboards in the bow. There was in total 165 bales of cannabis marijuana each weighing approximately 22 pounds, for a total of 3,640 pounds with an estimated street value exceeding $6.5 million.

MV Bakur.

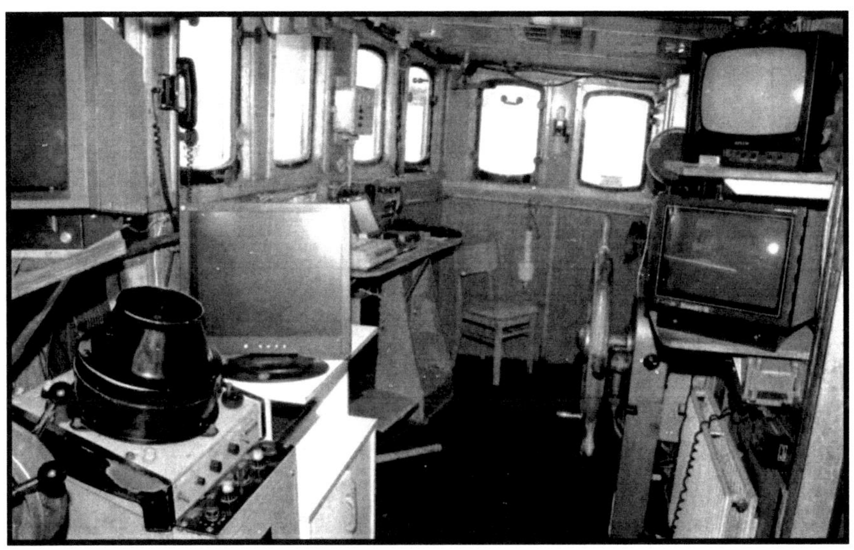

Wheelhouse of *MV Bakur.*

The 52 Step Dock stairs.

The 52 Steps Dock Marina in Ucluelet, B.C.

Main deck of *Bakur*.

The forward two holds of *Bakur*.

Cover removed from the forward hold.

Cover removed from the aft hold showing insulation.

Pot hidden behind *Bakur* panelling.

RCMP during media presentation.

Bakur arrest summary.

CHAPTER 23

Because the cops forced the Mexican, with no legal right to be on Canadian soil, off the ship the authorities had no choice but to extradite him to Mexico. But it didn't end there; the Immigration Department did everything they could to extract the cost of his flight from Ralph and Phil's already-empty pockets.

According to rumours drifting about, Phil and Ralph fared much better than the fellow who had set up the deal for them in Mexico. According to the media, "The Mexican, his wife, family and their maid, were all slaughtered by the cartel. Failure was a personal assault and, in every case, someone paid the ultimate price."

Phil takes exception to this sort of fake news as he views it. "No one died. The Cartel doesn't kill people at random. They know it's the cost of doing business. If you steal from them or rat them out, well, that's a different matter."

Arraignment for Ralph Harris, Phil Stirling and their crew was scheduled in Victoria for the following Wednesday.

John Green represented Phil and maintained his client's innocence from the beginning. "Even if the case went forward, Green felt we would have been acquitted," Phil says. Art Williams' legendary lawyer, Sid Simons, represented Ralph.

Stirling posted $10,000 bail, but it looked like Ralph would remain behind bars until the hearing as his finances were on life support. Forgotten and forsaken, no one seemed interested or able to bail him out. Definitely not his girlfriends, nor his business associates. It was his eldest daughter who finally came to the rescue by pulling a large chunk of cash out of her savings.

During the preliminary hearing of June 7, Green pointed out to the court that the RCMP had engaged the Department of Fisheries, along with Customs and Immigration Canada, to represent them as the initial boarding party. In doing so they rendered these two agencies as acting on behalf of the RCMP and therefore any warrant used to board and search the vessel needed to include them, which it didn't.

For Crown counsel Peter Hogg, that single act of stupidity rendered the case over before it began. He was forced to drop all charges rather than lose face in court. Following eight months of daily surveillance, countless manpower, including air travel, plus the expense of contractors to tow the vessel and remove its cargo, the case was closed.

With the help of lawyer Peter Ritchie, the courts returned the *Bakur* to Ralph and Phil on August 10 along with all their worldly possessions.

By some mysterious means, the $360,000 gained from the earlier fish sale, which had been hidden behind the forward bulkhead was never reported by the cops as part of their seizure, hence it was never returned. It was gone and none of the cops seemed to know anything about it. Ralph added, "Strange don't you think? There was no record at all of the money being entered onto the evidence manifest."

While all this legal wrestling was going on, the feds had towed the ship to the Annacis Island Marine Base on the Mainland in Delta. The boys were left with a ship having an appraised value of $2.2 million, plus 22,000 gallons of fuel in the tanks, only to find the market for ships of this type was nonexistent.

With no other option, Ralph and Phil sailed south to sell the *Bakur* to Phil's old friend in Mexico for ten cents on the dollar. This would at least offset their debt with him. By the time they paid off their remaining debts, they figured they would each take home $48,000.

Shawn Cochrane came on board before the final trip south, long enough to confirm everything was in good running order, after which he left for points unknown, leaving Phil and Ralph to their own devices. En route, 200 miles north of San Francisco, off Cape Mendocino, Phil realized he had water in the starboard fuel tank and insufficient fuel to make it to El Chapo's home port.

It turned out, their beloved engineer Shawn Cochrane had stolen the fuel in the starboard tank and filled it with water so the gauge would register full.

He also stole $2,000 out of Ralph's jacket pocket as it hung in his cabin. "I'd kill him if I could find him," Ralph said after learning of Cochrane's betrayal.

Phil says they were left with few options. "Since we both had criminal records, entering the U.S. by conventional means was out of the question. We had no choice but to call the American Tuna Association's lawyer for help in accessing the nearest U.S. port. Under International Maritime Law, no country could refuse us because of our situation.

"Not long after I got off the phone from the lawyer, out came a U.S. gunboat loaded with DEA and customs officials. They boarded and made it clear that we were going to be doing time, even though we had no drugs on board.

"As soon as we docked at Fisherman's Wharf in San Francisco, there had to be 150 guys going over every inch of our ship. They were all armed to the teeth. There were gun dogs and drug dogs, but they found nothing.

"Mark Shelly and Brodie Allen from ICE came on board once again and chased everyone else off. They did their best to convince us to work for them. They hammered us for two weeks until they had to finally concede there was nothing to hold us on. Just the same, they seized the *Bakur*, and gave us $2,500 with two airline tickets to fly home.

"The only consolation over that period in time was they brought us pizza once again.

"Peter Richie went after them for boarding without cause and seizing our ship without a warrant. Three weeks later, we flew back down and carried on to our destination."

Ralph Harris returned home a bitter man, trying desperately to find someone worthy of his trigger finger. He saw Phil and his wife as a common denominator in the loss of both the *Western Wind* and the *Bakur.* These were two ventures that would have scored well in his annals of history, yet both trips were utter failures.

He swore if the opportunity ever came his way, he would kill them both. Stirling sloughs off Ralph's threat. "Ralph has dispatched a number of people before their best before date, so I have no doubt he could carry out his threat. But when it comes to me he will have to stand in line. Life is trying to kill Marlene and I. Life is trying to kill everyone and it always succeeds. It's all a question as to how long we can cheat fate."

Ralph also saw Lea Sheppe as the primary individual behind the failures. Not only had he refused to call the *Western Wind* deal off when it was known the cops were on to them, he positioned himself in clear sight of the cops and announced his purpose at Cheanuh Marina on the day they were scheduled to land.

Ralph spent many evenings hidden in the bushes that lined Sheppe's driveway waiting for him to arrive home and then walk up within range of the front door. Fortunately for Lea, he never kept a regimented schedule when it came to his comings and goings and invariably when he did return, he always did so with a lady friend or a child, or both. If this were not the case, someone always opened the front door the moment he pulled into his driveway. Luck is the only reason Sheppe continues to walk the streets today. Ralph needed someone to vent on, so figuring his roommate Richie had stolen $150 from him, he convinced him to help dig a hole for some other poor schmuck. Little did he know that hole was to become his own final resting place. When it was deep enough, Ralph put a single round into the back of Richie's head, after which he told friends how he stood mesmerized by the fountain of dark red blood that shot up out of the hole with each heartbeat.

According to Phil Stirling, "Ralph also wanted to kill our mutual friend Mike Miller. Supposedly Mike had threatened Ralph over non-payment of a debt." That's a reminder of one lesson that Margaret Williams learned back in 1979. If you look forward to dying at some ripe old age and not before, you never threaten Ralph.

Where many would show strength in keeping such deeds quiet, Ralph told everyone in his inner circle of his homicidal deeds. Uncertain whether it was fear that kept them quiet or misguided respect, those same people are only now speaking after his passing.

As for Phil Stirling, he ended up working for Shelley and Brodie, not importing drugs north as originally discussed, but running guns to the Farc rebels in Honduras.

"These were small arms they had me carrying. There were hundreds of .50 calibre machine guns, rocket launchers and grenades. It was Oliver North's Iran Contra affair all over again."

Meanwhile, life and all the mayhem he had endured, was catching up with Ralph Harris. His financial situation had deteriorated significantly, and the taxman was on his case.

"My hair had started going grey about this time," noted Ralph in an interview late in his life, "but it turned completely white in the months that followed.

"Prior to our first trip to Mexico aboard the *Bakur,* Phil had convinced me to grant his wife Marlene power-of-attorney over my assets so that she could manage my affairs while I was at sea or if something should detain us for any number of reasons. I had done a few deals with Phil, so I had no reason to distrust him. I met with their lawyer and signed the document.

"While we were at sea, Marlene took a $100,000 mortgage out against my home before my first month of absence had passed. Then she took a second private mortgage leveraging my home for in excess of half a million dollars. She claims the money was necessary to finance the trip, but I never saw a dollar of their savings going into that voyage. By the time I got home it was painfully clear I had been financially screwed.

"On April 14, 2011, Revenue Canada declared I owed them $320,246.28 for unpaid taxes on revenue they presumed I earned with my grow-op. How odd it is that the feds claim rights to a portion of the money I earned from the illegal drug trade while the same government is eager to throw me in jail for the deed while seizing all my assets as proceeds of crime.

"Anyway, the bank sent me notice by registered mail that they were demanding repayment of the loan the Stirlings took out against my house, while this other fellow who lent them $400,000 was screaming for full payment as well. The only option I had left was to sell the place and hopefully clear my losses. Whatever remained, Rev Canada grabbed before it could reach my pocket.

"So here I was bankrupt without a pot to piss in. I shouldn't be too upset as the home cost me $250,000 to build and I did it with drug money. And I had made a lot of money off of it. On the other hand, it was my home, and I was comfortable there.

"Phil insisted he was broke as well but I find that hard to accept. I'm pretty certain he has vast sums of money squirreled away somewhere safe. He still has his home, his fish plant, his ship, *Equalizer,* and all the toys in the world a man could desire. To the best of my knowledge, none have a mortgage against them. If this is a definition of being broke, I will trade places any day of the week.

"With everything that has happened, I don't know how it is that Phil has lived so long. I was certain the bikers would have wanted to settle a score after he tried to sell them out for a million bucks. I swear if I live long enough, I will bury both him and his wife so deep no one will find them."

Fortunately for Phil Stirling and Marlene, that day never came.

CHAPTER 24

They say bad things come in threes, but there is no justifiable reason why that theory needed to play out in Ralph's case. Nonetheless, not long after the *Bakur* fiasco, the cops raided his ecstasy lab in Nanoose.

"I lawyered up once again and the matter went to court and I was represented by one of Canada's primo criminal defense lawyers, Ken Westlake.

"The prosecution never had its chance to serve up their overly rehearsed questions, nor plow through the statistics shadowing the recent rise in drug trafficking or the increase in the number of teenagers who are buying and selling my stuff."

Without delay, Westlake exercised the skill of a true artist having the charges thrown out without much ado.

"Ken demonstrated to the judge that the cops had illegally tapped my partner's phone and that in itself was grounds for dismissal."

The grim-faced prosecutor could do nothing but stand there frowning.

Ken Westlake is a great lawyer if you are deemed to be on the wrong side of the law. He has often been accused of presenting misinformation or putting positive spins on negative events to win his clients a get-free card. More than once he would drag out a scheduled five-week trial to five months to win a dismissal by presenting more motions than Carter has little liver pills.

He's no small-time criminal defense lawyer and has represented various members of the Hells Angels and the entire club from time to time when he would artistically paint the arresting cops as "junior officers not knowing what they were doing". Without fail, the ploy always generated the desired public outcry about cops wasting time and taxpayer money on small street-level drug arrests.

One such ploy saw two Calgary cops charged and the police brass apologizing for the way they handled HA member Jason Arkinstall's case in 2009 as Westlake turned Justice Kathleen Ganley's attention towards the credibility of the cops' testimony.

An internal administrative review ordered both cops to take counselling for their failure to take adequate notes. Westlake wasn't satisfied until the matter had been referred to the Alberta Serious Incident Response Team in 2014. They in turn recommended criminal charges against the two cops, reporting the case is "Reflective of a seriously dysfunctional police service that for decades has failed to adequately address police misconduct from within its ranks." Both cops were formally charged in 2017.

Arkinstall was acquitted of uttering threats, obstruction of justice and assault and that was all Westlake was after.

"It is reasons such as this that I chose to have Ken in my corner if my case went to trial," Ralph explained.

The trial involving Ralph's lab didn't end with his acquittal, as the Crown immediately appealed the ruling and this time the feds won. Not willing to leave it at that, Ralph instructed Westlake to take the matter to the B.C. Supreme Court. There, the seven justices acknowledged that the prosecution had denied Ralph and his lawyer access to the packet used to justify the wiretap warrant and therefore gave the prosecution an unfair advantage in the case.

They also acknowledged that with the defense's inability to access the packet, they were unable to determine for themselves whether the justification needed to gain the warrant fell within the perimeters of the law. At the end of the hearing the Supreme Court ruled: "When it comes to interception of private communications – withholding evidence leading up to the issuance of a warrant, inclusive of said warrant from the defense, when the resulting wiretap is key to the prosecution's evidence, deprives the defense of its ability to conclude that the warrant was granted in accordance to the measures of law, plus make full answer and defense.

"Unless the prosecution can demonstrate the accused showed prima facie misconduct before the wiretap is authorized, according to the Charter of Rights and Freedoms, the evidence accrued from the wiretap shall be ruled inadmissible."

Following that trial, Ken Westlake presented a writ before the Supreme Court of Canada which eventually rendered wiretapping illegal unless authorized in advance by a judge. "With this new legislation and the connections some of my associates had within the courts, we would in all likelihood know when our phones were going to be tapped and could ensure nothing was said that would cause us difficulty.

"Sid Simons was another counsel of choice for many in my position. He worked hard and treated everyone fairly. Unlike many of his peers, I was free to call him at home or on a weekend if needed. He even made house calls or in a couple of cases, jail calls. He referred to himself as a street lawyer, an advocate for clients who worked in factories, who got injured or discriminated against, or who ran afoul of the law, as was often my case. His clients were not banks or insurance companies or real estate agencies. They were common folks who sometimes could ill afford legal fees. Sid viewed the practice of law as a calling, a mission to help those less fortunate. He was so successful that throughout the judicial system he became known as 'Slippery Sid'.

While Ralph may have won the case, it didn't result in business as usual. The system had no intention of returning his needed supplies or equipment so he would have to start from square one. Finding a suitable location to work out of is never easy. Logistics play a major role. It has to be tucked beyond prying eyes, yet accessible enough to permit ease of coming and going. Just the same, the return on the investment is so great, in Ralph's mind it was worth the effort.

CHAPTER 25

In his final weeks, Ralph Harris reflected on his life; the good times and the bad. As was his habit throughout his life, he held little back when conversing with people he trusted. Trust was essential given the material Ralph had to share.

"Following fifty years of exile, my first wife Yvonne decided to resurface and work her way back into my life. I'm not exactly clear as to what her endgame was but the time we've had together since her return has been pleasant for the most part. While she has gained a few extra pounds, much like the rest of us, she still retains some of her girlish charm.

"I can no longer remember when I last had sex and the longer I dwell on it, the more consumed I am by the thought.

"My mating rituals, the stalking, the accidental encounters, the extravagant gifts, the awkward phone calls, no longer have a familiar outcome. I've never lied about who I am to any of them, but what I have been for the past decade is written across my face like a neon sign reading, 'Old, worn out, busted'. My youthful innocence vanished half a century ago and has been replaced with a street-hardened core that would shake most any seasoned social worker.

"It matters not how long or wide a man's appendage is. Age is an equalizer for us all. Instinctively my eyes continue to engage every gorgeous woman, young or old, who will offer me the time of day, in hopes of getting into her pants. But indifference between the past and present is the outcome. No longer do their rejections soften with each approach until they weaken and finally acquiesce. The game of courtship for most occasions is passé.

"Having said that, the age-old game routinely played out between men and women still happened from time to time, but it is no longer with women somewhat my junior. It is with those where life has reduced their features to clearly reflect that of my own.

"They struggle to employ their old flirtatious persona as a matter of course, which for the most part I find flattering, somewhat irresistible and then noticeably untouchable as they withdraw. But in reality, it falls flat today and at times appears ridiculous and degrading not only to myself as a willing participant, but to them who have much more than a sexy image to offer a relationship.

"As to those who I have spent time with, I confess, I continue to fantasize over the past. Each have aged chronologically, much like myself, but for the most part Mother Nature has shown them kindness as they have retained many of their girlish attributes allowing them to migrate towards greener pastures, somewhat their junior. The day when offers of unlimited pot or cocaine drew willing vixens through my bedroom door is, sadly, all a matter of history.

"All those tight little bodies are nothing but a memory. The sound of girlish laughter echoing through my house has faded off somewhere into the drywall. Their enticing fragrance is lost to points I don't know, all of which confirms life can be cruel.

"While I have been less than a perfect husband, I have never trash-talked Kathy to anyone, not before or after our separation. Yet I can't help but think my present state is karma for all those times I cheated on her and our kids.

"Genetically, I was blessed with having solid features without forcing me to hit the gym on a regular basis but all that started to change when I looked in the mirror and realized the negative effects of old age.

"While driving home, not long back, a swallow darted in front of my truck and was almost clipped by a car passing in the opposite direction. In a millisecond, with a twist of its body it soared up and out of the way only to be swept away on a breeze. I found it an epiphany of sorts as I believe that swallow is much like myself.

"Since my youth I have been addicted, not to the drugs I sell, but rather to the need to defy the law, only to find myself close to losing my freedom and invariably catch a break and fly away to repeat the stunt all over again. The loss of my family was never enough to effect a positive change. The high was simply too great to resist.

"In my later years I searched desperately for the right balance between that which drove me forward in my career of choice and my desire to be a good father and husband. But I was left time and again with the question: Could there ever be a perfect balance between what I felt compelled to do versus what I knew I needed to do?

"A few miles north of Ladysmith was my lab, pushing out millions of dollars in social drugs each year. Just outside the front door of my Ladysmith home I had my grow-op, churning out half a million a year, and yet down the road a mile or so lived Kathy and my family, waiting patiently for me to recognize what I was missing.

"I never used to have difficulty sleeping. I would just stare at reruns of Hogan's Heroes night after night until I dropped off. Now I lay awake for hours staring at the ceiling, praying that fatigue will take over and I will drop off for at least a couple of hours each night.

"In my world, enemies are ruthless. If I make nice, I get crushed. Certain members of the RCMP and even some of those who wear a patch denoting the most feared criminal organization in the world suggest I am a man to be feared. But I can assure you; I am not a sociopathic killer. When I took a life, I did so out of necessity or on behalf of those who considered it a necessary part of their work protocol. And only when there appeared no reasonable alternative.

"There have been a number of times when lethal force has not been required. On an occasion, people have felt it necessary to threaten a member of my family. In most cases I have found a heart-to-heart talk with those individuals has assisted them in realizing their choices may not be in their best interests.

"There are now occasions when I wake during the night in a cold sweat with some nightmare portraying Margaret Williams or any of the other poor souls I've dispatched early to whatever their individual eternity represented. I have no reason to doubt one of these nightmares will place sufficient pressure on my heart that my life will slip away while I sleep. For those who have wondered, I've never wasted much time thinking about heaven or hell. But I guess time will tell if there is some form of divine justice.

"I've spent a life looking over my shoulder trying to discern if the individual sitting behind the wheel of the dark non-descript sedan is a narc or just a person who was budget conscience and not willing to waste their hard-earned money on splashy paint and chrome wheels. The small antenna perched on the rear fender of a cop's car was once a giveaway but in more recent years their communication systems are blended into the front or rear windshield rendering them near invisible.

"I've already survived one heart attack which led to a quintuple bypass. Recovery was good but the physician made it clear it may be an indication of what's to come. Although I only had the occasional Bud Light, I did smoke far too many joints and partook in a whole lot more sex than the average man requires, all of which has now taken its toll.

"In my heyday, science never recognized that the high pressure sodium light I used to encourage plant growth would one day leave me with macular degeneration and damage to my cornea. I wore the recommended colour-corrected lenses but only after experience rendered it a necessity. I can only imagine what state I would be in if I employed the practice of pumping carbon dioxide into my barn like they do today to accelerate growth. With time, the chemists have found that low levels can be harmless to a worker, but too high a level has proven toxic causing asphyxiation to some during the early trials.

"I now have no choice but to wear these coke-bottled glasses as the onslaught of glaucoma has slowly crept into each eye. I have had no option but to forfeit my driver's license, hence I can no longer move freely about to generate an income, thus leaving me at the mercy of the one lady that I deserve the least to chauffer me where I need to go. A few select friends have volunteered to drive me to an occasional conjugal visit with my first wife or other longsuffering girlfriend. But other than them, I am at the mercy of Kathy or one of my daughters."

By some curious twist of fate, over the years, on thirteen different occasions, Ralph Harris wiggled through the judicial cracks avoiding the charges brought against him. But that matters little as he lost his home and property in the end to bad ventures and the tax man.

With the passing of the new C-24 legislation in January 2014, it's become much harder to evade prosecution. This new paper is much like the RICO Act in the States whereby you are guilty by mere association. It also reduced the legal definition of a criminal organization to three members with a wider range of discretion to render it an offence for any person to be knowingly associated with a criminal organization.

Under this new law, a lawyer or an accountant representing a criminal organization could be found complicit or guilty. The same for a private contractor acting as a bodyguard or possibly a padre taking a confession. Each are treated as an equal to the man wearing his colors for all to see.

As absurd as it may sound, if the Hells Angels were ever inclined to take in a club chaplin, that man of the cloth would be subject to incarceration even though his sole desire was to see the very men under his charge change their lives for the better.

"I figure some future owner of my home is going to get a hell of a surprise if he or she ever decides to make major renovations. I had a number of firearms that needed to be kept out of the authorities' hands, so I hid them behind the drywall in a certain room. I knew where they were and could retrieve them at a moment's notice. The cost of a drywall patch and a dab of paint was cheap insurance they would not be found. I'm not going to say which room they are in as that would take the fun out of it for anyone who goes looking.

"As for my home, Rev Canada makes up their own rules as they go. Had Ken Westlake been acting on my behalf as he did for another fellow in a similar situation, the feds would have been the loser, not me.

"They have a unique way of assessing you for perceived income earned from your involvement in the drug trade. Nothing is more ironic than to be declared a criminal for transporting, cultivating, and selling a social drug that some piece of legislation states is illegal, unless that is, it is prescribed by a physician. Then after the matter has wound its way through the courts, even if you are acquitted, they still want their piece of the pie, illegal money or not.

"Being homeless as I was, Kathy took pity on me and offered me her master bedroom; but not with her in it. Her being there would have been nice, but nonetheless a bed with a roof over it is still far better than my other options. She still jogs and maintains a trim athletic body because of it, but I seldom see her smile. For all that she has been through and all that she is doing for me, she is a saint who long after I'm gone, will remain so.

"Some will consider me a vile person who snuffed out lives or destroyed marriages through the production and importation of illicit drugs. While my own take on the subject is somewhat different, I will at least go on record as saying I produced primarily marijuana, MDA and MDMA, all of which is considered today to be social drugs. Unlike meth, crack, acid, PCP and so many others, my drugs were not addictive and did not generate hallucinations but rather a warm buzz that suppresses or heightens the senses. In contrast, had I not imported the volume of cocaine that I did, someone else would have. Rather a weak defence I guess, but the only one I have.

"If I have any regret in life, it is thinking about Kathy now uncovering the truth about the man she married and what his life really consisted of. She knew of my grow-ops and the odd small deal, but I never troubled her with the bigger transactions or any of the murders. Knowledge of those would not have been good for her well-being and besides they were well beyond her need-to-know.

"I can joke now like Flip Wilson's show of the '70s: 'The devil made me do it.' But in reality, God forgive me, she deserved so much more.

"Kathy does not need to worry about those parts of my past that should never be spoken of, as I never committed anything to a cell phone memory or a computer hard drive."

Ralph Harris knew his life story would be eventually told in a book and near the end of his life he stated, "anything of consequence that is not found between these pages has been retained solely within my memory, which unfortunately has suffered a few too many glitches over the past few years."

Ralph Harris has never been a man in need of possessions but now he is in need of nothing, short of a Divine resurrection.

ACKNOWLEDGEMENTS

It is said, "some books write themselves, while others want the words to be wrestled onto the page."

I have personally found that each book I've written has been a product of the latter rather than the former.

Those which I have penned have evolved after investing thousands of hours of investigation, interviews, and documental research. But while that has always been the case, none could exist if it were not for the trust and commitment of those who knew the subject firsthand and demonstrated a willingness to share their personal knowledge without reservation.

Many of those who opened up to share insight into their lives, sought no form of recognition, however, Ralph Harris may be the sole exception.

Ralph Ross Harris gave birth to the book *Nobody's Boy - The Northern Connection* while I was completing a series of interviews with his first wife Yvonne. I had previously interviewed Ralph regarding his involvement in the Art Williams story and he in turn introduced me to Yvonne, feeling the brutality she endured as an infant at the hands of her mother needed to be exposed.

At the time I never approached the subject of Ralph's life other than his early years with Yvonne, as I knew him to be an extremely guarded individual and, in all likelihood, would take to his grave far more than he would ever divulge.

Surprisingly that didn't stop him from throwing out the idea. He had a conviction that his life was worth recording, albeit with the adjunct that it couldn't go to print prior to his passing.

Ralph and I met on several occasions in his reserved booth at the rear of the Haida Way Restaurant in Chemainus. It was not a classy place, but one that was known to broker a number of deals between an equal number of shady characters, where shelter from unwanted ears and roaming eyes could be attained and where staff knew not to linger at his table or ask questions.

He had his booth staked out in the far corner where he could keep his back to the wall, an eye out the window to monitor those approaching the building, and the other reading the intent of those who came through the front door. If needed, he could make a quick exit behind the counter and through the kitchen to the rear of the building.

While Ralph registered a degree of concern over exposing those he had worked with, I have taken it one step further and held back those names which may compromise the comfort and well-being of his family.

Some of Ralph's extended family opened their doors to me and welcomed the opportunity to see the life of their husband, father, and brother, gain literary light. They each acknowledged that this book may expose elements of Ralph that could prove embarrassing or in some cases shocking, but nonetheless they wanted to move forward and see where it would lead. Rather than mention each by name, I will let it be sufficient to express my gratitude for the unparalleled contribution of their memories, personal effects, court documents and photos.

Nobody's Boy gained immeasurable depth, verisimilitude, and complexity from the input of those who worked and played with him over the past fifty years.

A special thanks to Trish for sharing her experiences as one of Ralph's many love interests. Your open, unabashed segment of his life has enabled me to understand the deeper turmoil that infested his marriage and family life.

Likely the greatest contribution to this book comes from Ralph's partner in crime, John Philip Stirling, for he had not only opened the inner door of his life but provided me with boxes of evidence the authorities had gathered during their investigation into his and Ralph's life together.

As part of my thanks, I would be remiss if I didn't draw your attention to Phil's personal memoirs entitled *The Last Pirate* which is currently in circulation as a Kindle four-book series. This is a must read for any true crime enthusiast.

As with my book *85 Grams* and the quest to take down Art Williams, Pat Convey once again opened his archival memory to the details surrounding the *Western Wind* and the debacle that followed. Wayne Flewelling did likewise as he spearheaded the second prong attempt at bringing justice to that which Inspector Richard Barszczewski so carelessly scuttled. Lastly, Terry Illingworth exposed the behind-the-scenes action that led to the taking down of the *Western Wind* and other such ventures.

To allow this book to come to life, the principal characters not only donated countless hours, but revealed the risks and obstacles that they had to overcome to play their part.

As with most authors, my work would not be possible without the patience granted to me by my life partner. In my case, my wife falls squarely behind the crosshairs of my work, being not only the patient bystander, but the first-line editor for my lack of good spelling and grammar.

WHERE ARE THEY NOW?

• **Ralph Ross Harris** continued to do what he knew best at the close of the *Bakur* affair, but he never again accumulated the wealth he once had. As his health failed, he restricted his activities to brokering deals for others in the trade. On December 5, 2017 he succumbed to heart failure in the middle of the night at the age of 78.

• **Yvonne (Harris) Fantin**, Ralph's first wife, returned to Vancouver Island where she reinserted herself into Ralph's life. During a recent interview, she seemed lucid at first, even though she refused to speak of Ralph or herself, but proceeded to rely on two imaginary friends she called 'Mutt and Jeff' to guide her thoughts. It was hard at times to discern when reality vacated her conversation, for that which was surreal. She is now bedridden and lives out her senior years in a care home.

• **Kathy Harris**, Ralph's wife retired from the Cowichan Hospital and became Ralph's caregiver during his declining years. With more than ample reason to speak poorly of him, she has never uttered an ill word. Her dedication to him in his final years was unconditional, just the same she would rather push those years where he repaid her love with Hell on Earth, so far back in her mind, they never become a source of conversation.

• **John Philip Stirling** continued to ferry shiploads of drugs from Mexico and South America into the Pacific Northwest and points beyond. His success rate remained in the high 90s but he did have two interdictions that cost him a short residency in a U.S. prison.

> •On Oct. 18, 2011, he was apprehended aboard the sailboat *Atlantis V* while off the coast of Venezuela, en route to Australia. He had 381 kilos of cocaine secreted away. He

received a seven-and-a-half-year sentence in a U.S. prison reserved for non-nationals.

•On April 9, 2019 his ship *Mandalay* was boarded off Newport, Oregon while 225 nautical miles deep in international waters. He was heading north with 28 barrels of liquid methamphetamine and a substantial quantity of fentanyl from Mexico for the Pacific Northwest bikers. He received a 34-month sentence in a U.S. prison.

•Released July 5, 2021, Phil is in good health and residing in the Gulf Islands. He is between jobs while self-publishing his memoirs *The Last Pirate* as a four-book series.

•He and his wife Marlene have gone their separate ways, while his son Beau has become a man seeking his own identity.

• **Shawn Cochrane** is presumed to be breathing free air, but his current location is unknown.

• **John William Green** – Stirling's lawyer passed away in Victoria Nov. 23, 2018 of leukemia at the age of 66, well before his time.

• **Jennifer Eileen McCormick** – Stirling's lawyer is still practicing, but has faced her own judicial demons, with her license suspended in 2014 for disclosing client information.

• **Ken Westlake** – Harris's lawyer is now semi-retired on the Mainland.

• **Sgt. Pat Convey** – is enjoying his well-earned retirement on the Saanich Peninsula, just outside Victoria, B.C.

•Today he remains inflamed over how his superiors threw him and his peers under the bus after engineering what may have been the greatest drug bust in Canadian history.

•While never uttering the words, he can't help but ponder whether the superior who scuttled the deal had more than a casual relationship with his former RCMP partner 'Savoie' who took his own life after being convicted of corruption.

- **David Francis Watt** (Convey's partner) – passed away Aug. 14, 2010, at the age of 78.

- **David Giles aka Gyrator** – passed away July 2017 of liver failure in the Abbotsford hospital, three months after being handed a record sentence for his role in a massive cocaine conspiracy.

- **Lea Sheppe** – retired from the Nanaimo bikers, while he continues to ride the open road on his government pensions.

OF INTEREST

Not long after the RCMP files covering the investigation into the *Western Wind* closed, John Philip Stirling registered a formal complaint against the RCMP through his Vancouver lawyer Peter Ritchie for their treatment of him, and especially how Inspector Richard Barszczewski left him exposed to biker retaliation.

As with all complaints, the matter was turned over to Internal Affairs where, as a general rule, such complaints receive a cursory once over and are then filed with a nice thank you letter being sent off to the complainant. "In this particular case," reports Sgt. Wayne Flewelling, "alarm bells went off with every page of the *Western Wind* investigation.

"I met with Stirling and his lawyer, as the former agreed to tell all, provided he was given immunity from everything he offered, in addition to supporting his legal fees. Nothing else. The $1 million he demanded earlier was off the table. In my view, he was being as honest and above board as possible for him, so I drafted up a letter of agreement which he signed under his lawyer's supervision.

"Phil was known as a bona fide smuggler and in our opinion, he would likely offend again, so I cautioned him that if he was caught in the act, the deal was off.

"I took the matter to the then Chief Prosecutor Martha Devlin, who after a brief minute or two of consideration, refused to accept the deal, stating 'Stirling would never be viewed in court as a credible witness'.

"I couldn't believe what I was hearing. Not only had Barszczewski scuttled the greatest opportunity this country had seen in the history of drug enforcement and for unexplained reasons, but here Devlin followed his lead.

"It would have cost the government roughly $20,000 in legal fees and this guy would have delivered to us those money men back east living comfortably at the top of the ladder, plus the ones who engineered the largest known cocaine delivery in the history of the Pacific Northwest.

"Everyone involved in the case surrounding Stirling and the *Western Wind* questioned the possibility of corruption within the upper ranks when the original case went south, and then this happened with Devlin. You just gotta wonder."

To this day Barszczeski refuses to offer any insight into why he seemed to be protecting the interests of the criminal element masterminding the multi-billion-dollar Canadian drug trade.

"This story line that Flewelling is feeding is nothing more than a load of crap," says Stirling. "I enjoy life far too much to roll on the bikers. As for the deal with Convey, that is far more grey than black and white.

"Indeed, I did have discussions with Convey about serving up the bikers on a silver platter, but it was only to provide me with a get-out-of-jail card should things go south. We knew before we set sail that the cops were onto us but the bikers insisted we proceed just the same.

"Would I have exercised that deal to burn the most feared organized crime group in the world? Not a chance. Had I wanted to do that, there was plenty of opportunity within the eighteen days of confinement the RCMP held me under following my extradition from the States."

"While I don't necessarily support the conversations Phil had with the cops," Ralph Harris told the author, "It did appear to be the right move at the time."

"We knew there was a rat embedded at some level in the bikers, we just didn't know where. It wasn't until well after the fact that we learned he was well-connected with the Montreal club and had been selling biker information since the early 1990s and may still be operating today. The cops could not afford to waste such a valued asset by exposing him as a witness during a trial, so they needed someone who was expendable when the dust had cleared, and Phil was their man."

The court of public opinion has always been in flux. What had once been considered a threat to humanity prior to recent years has now been sanctioned for legal distribution under municipal license. For those who found themselves serving time for simple possession of pot in years past, their bitterness must echo through the halls of justice today.

Ralph Harris came to know a fair number of the local and Mainland cops over the years. Most he had no use for but there were a couple who did their job while showing him respect, making them worthy, in his opinion, of the badge they wore.

Unfortunately, some professions are breeding grounds for certain personalities. Sadistic individuals will be drawn towards police or prosecutorial work as it offers them an easy target to exercise their aggression without fear of reprisal.

We have all encountered the cowboys or schoolyard bullies who wave a badge, without which they would find it difficult to function within the adult world. They strut around with their chest pumped out and a proverbial chip on their shoulder, making threats with every confrontation.

They have never been shy about fabricating evidence in order to get a bust and if that were insufficient to bolster a case in court, they will pay experts-for-hire to give testimony about details that are non-existent.

The fallacy of the legal system condemns the defense attorneys to jail time if they're caught straying from the truth while under oath. Yet the rules seem to be much less onerous when it comes to the prosecution side.

There are times when a cop will step over that thin blue line of what is right and forget which side of the law he or she is sworn to protect. This happens frequently with those working undercover and while Ralph appreciated some of the cops because their incompetence helped him navigate through the cracks in the court system so many times, he detested them for their moral low ground. As they say: Cops and politicians can be bought for a dollar on Monday and traded for favours on Tuesday.

Their first transgression can be as innocent as taking a free cup of coffee. No big thing: they just get a wee bit too cozy with the underbelly of society and are offered a cup to settle their nerves or reward them for all the crap they go through in the course of a day. With time the cycle weakens until their on/off switch morphs into a dimmer switch.

Once over that line, their lust for easy money or the lure that comes with being associated with the bad guys makes them an easy target. What follows is their inability to recognize when the switch has been thrown from good cop to questionable cop.

EPILOGUE

The story of Ralph Ross Harris is perplexing at best. There is no question he was bred with an ample supply of street smarts. Having conducted himself as he had for the better part of sixty years while managing to shrink away from having been charged over a dozen times with not a single conviction, his is not the legacy of many career criminals.

To have murdered so many men and women and never once been charged is either judicial impunity for the greater good, an outrageous illustration of the RCMP's incompetence or his inconceivable ability to function outside the arms of law.

Clearly, the Canadian authorities are not overly interested in ridding the streets of drugs, nor are they focused on taking down those who bring the drugs onto our shores. If this were not true, the overseeing of our ports would remain in the hands of a prejudicial policing system. Also, the ability to curtail the flow of large quantity of drugs when they are intercepted would not be hampered by the upper echelons.

As Ralph put it, "I don't think they wanted to stop the flow of drugs as it would put too many people out of jobs. Judges, cops, lawyers, politicians, prison personnel, probation officers. The flow employs too many people. If they stopped the drugs coming into the country, there would be 100,000 people out of a job overnight. The authorities have long learned that to take me out would only create a vacuum into which some other dude would flow. My kind is a long way from finding itself on the endangered species list."

One has to ask: Was there more to Ralph's story than what has been told? It is written: 'Sociopaths are incapable of guilt or shame for their actions; they don't feel remorse as they are only concerned with their own interests.'

Who really was Ralph Ross Harris?

BIBLIOGRAPHY

- *(Seattle)Times Newspaper*
- *Times-Colonist Newspaper*
- *The Vancouver Sun*
- *B.C. Provincial Archives*

NON-PUBLISHED INTERVIEWS

- Ralph Ross Harris
- Natasha (Harris) Maquire
- John Philip Stirling
- Sgt. Pat Convey
- Staff Sgt. Terry Illingworth
- Sgt. Wayne Flewelling
- Michael O'Shea

PUBLISHED:

• Sher, Julian & Marsden, William, *The Road to Hell*. Vintage Canada, 2004

ABOUT THE AUTHOR

Daryl Ashby has developed a reputation for searching out subjects hitherto poorly analyzed or scarcely recorded, capturing unnoticed details that could possibly change public perception, as well as the implausible landscapes that our minds conveniently map.

As a local historian and journalist, he takes great pride ensuring his work is as accurate as possible, cutting no corners when it comes to digging at the truth while refusing to shelter those who warrant exposure for their past no matter what the risk.

If you enjoyed this read, you may also enjoy his first-person account *John Muir: West Coast Pioneer*, published by Ronsdale Press. This book provides an engaging account of the first 30 years in the Colony of Vancouver's Island, the foundation for what later became known as British Columbia, Canada. No other man singularly contributed as much to establish the settlement of the Pacific Northwest.

Daryl Ashby's presentation of John Muir's life and his related activities in and around the colony has been suitably recognized as a runner-up to the prestigious B.C. Book Prize as well as the Victoria-Butler Book Prize.

As a prequel to *Nobody's Boy*, the life story of Art Williams in *85 Grams: Art Williams –Drug Czar*, will provide you with an understanding of how Ralph Harris gained some of his first-hand knowledge of the world of synthetic drugs.

The story follows Art Williams from his youth through his war years and to a young man who morphed into one who despised all forms of authority. As a final jab at those who wished to throttle his freedom, he re-energized the use of the so-called love drug, MDA and populated the West Coast from California to Alaska with his product. As the cops tightened the noose around his freedom, he vanished, never to be seen again.